Panama, The Canal And The United States

Guides to Contemporary Issues

Richard Dean Burns, Editor

This series is devoted to exploring contemporary social, political, economic, diplomatic and military issues. Each volume contains an extended narrative which introduces opinions and interpretations relating to the issue under discussion and concludes with a bibliographical survey of essential writings on the topic.

#1 THE MX CONTROVERSY
Robert A. Hoover

#2 THE MILITARY IN THE DEVELOPMENT PROCESS
Nicole Ball

#3 THE PERSIAN GULF & UNITED STATES POLICY
Bruce R. Kuniholm

#4 CENTRAL AMERICA & UNITED STATES POLICIES,
1920s—1980s
Thomas M. Leonard

#5 THE PALESTINIAN PROBLEM & UNITED STATES
POLICY
Bruce R. Kuniholm & Michael Rubner

#6 FAMINE: A HERITAGE OF HUNGER
Arline T. Golkin

#7 THE STRATEGIC DEFENSE INITIATIVE
Douglas C. Waller, James T. Bruce & Douglas M. Cook

#8 AMERICA AND THE IRAQI CRISIS, 1990-1992
Lester H. Brune

#9 PANAMA, THE CANAL AND THE UNITED STATES
Thomas M. Leonard

Panama, The Canal and The United States:

A Guide to Issues and References

Thomas M. Leonard

REGINA BOOKS
Claremont, California

10   9   8   7   6   5   4   3   2   1

Library of Congress Cataloging-in-Publication Data

Leonard, Thomas M., 1937-
    Panama, the canal, and the United States : a guide to issues and references / Thomas M. Leonard.
        p. 132 cm. -- (Guides to contemporary issues ; #9)
    Includes bibliographical references (p. 121).
    ISBN 0-941690-55-5 (cloth) : $21.95. -- ISBN 0-941690-56-3 (pbk.) $11.95
    1. United States--Foreign relations--Panama. 2. Panama--Foreign relations--United States. 3. Panama Canal (Panama) I. Title. II. Series.
    E183.8.P2L384   1993
    327.7307287--dc20   93-26255
                                                        CIP

Regina Books
Post Office Box 280
Claremont, California 91711

Manufactured in the United States of America.

To Steve and Tom Bailey:
For Teaching Us The Meaning of Courage

CONTENTS

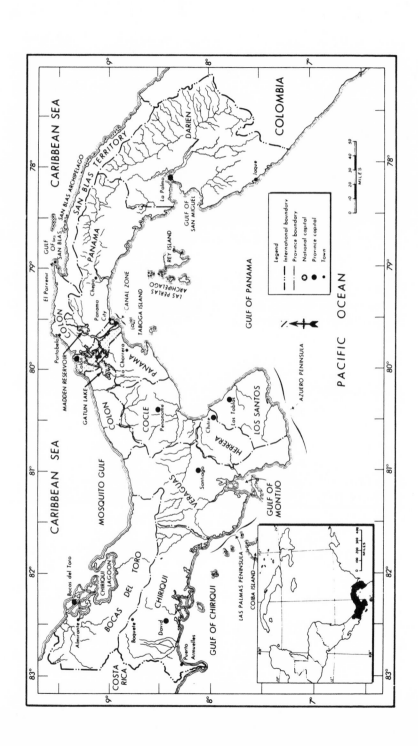

FOREWORD

In 1513, the Spanish conquistador Vasco Nuñez de Balboa marched across the isthmus at Panama and discovered that only a narrow strip of land separated the Atlantic and Pacific Oceans. From then until now, the isthmus of Panama has been a crossroad for international passenger and cargo traffic. Although Balboa's fellow conquistador Hernán Cortés envisioned a transisthmian canal, and in 1524 King Charles V of Spain ordered the first official survey of the region for a possible canal, it would be nearly 400 years before a canal linked the two oceans. When the Panama Canal opened on August 15, 1914, one week after the outbreak of World War I, it represented an unmatched engineering feat at the time.

Panama long served as a strategic locale in Spain's overseas empire and its people enjoyed special privileges in return. Until the eighteenth century, virtually all of Spain's trade with the west coast of South America had been transported across the isthmus and the port cities boasted modern fortifications. The Panamanian officials, who were paid well out of customhouse revenues, thought themselves destined to be the directors of international commerce and petitioned the king to establish a board of trade in their capital. But, beginning in the 1730s, trade slumped, and the once opulent fairs at Portobelo virtually ended. Increased shipping around Cape Horn, greater commerce with non-Spanish vessels (that is, contraband) and the trade liberalization allowed in the 1770s contributed to Panama's decline. Spain's mercantilist system no longer benefitted Panama and it soon became an outpost of empire.

Virtually no natural affinities existed between the United States and Panama prior to the latter's independence in 1903. The scant U.S. merchandise that landed at Panama in the 1790s and early 1800s usually was handled by resident British merchants. Panama, itself, had little to sell the world and most U.S. trade at the time was with Europe, the Caribbean and Brazil.

Like all Latin America, Panama was caught in the viscitudes of European intrigue that eventually led to its independence in 1821. In November of that year, the leading landowners and merchants declared their independence from Spain and annexation to Simón Bolívar's Gran Colombia. The new government at Bogotá moved quickly to protect the interests of Panama's elite. A commercial regulation authorized Panama, Portobelo and Chagre to trade freely with ships of friendly and neutral nations. It established rules for arrival and handling of cargo and sought to suppress contraband. This short-lived law revealed the Panamanians' desires to promote free trade and foster closer relations with former Spanish Colonies. Subsequently, Bolívar envisioned the construction of a railroad across the isthmus to link the two oceans. Although the North American built railroad that opened in 1855 brought little wealth to the isthmian state, the Panamanians continued to anticipate prosperity from a transisthmian canal.

In the late nineteenth century, the Panamanian leadership came to despise the government at Bogotá and recognized that their most precious resource, a transisthmian canal route, could help them achieve independence. At the same time, sentiment in the United States came to demand that Washington undertake an interoceanic canal project. The path between the seas brought Panama and the United States together in 1903. In return for making the republic's independence secure, the United States obtained the right to construct, operate, maintain and defend the canal at Panama.

With the canal's completion, the United States completed the greatest construction project the world had ever seen. Although no distinctly new engineering techniques were used in cutting the 51.2 mile channel, the scale of the undertaking was unprecedented. The original plan was to build a sea level canal, but that changed when the task of cutting through hard rock seemed too formidable. Between 1907 and 1913 the project's chief engineer, Army Colonel George W. Goethals, directed steam shovels, dynamite, loading trains and nearly 35,000 workers to excavate more than 232 million cubic yards of rock and earth from the bed of the canal. The local dams and other concrete construction contained about 4.8 million cubic yards of cement.

The North Americans also overcame tropical disease. Army Colonel William Gorgas, chief sanitary officer, introduced modern sanitation and public health procedures in 1904. Medical scientists discovered that yellow fever and malaria were carried by mosquitos. Widespread draining of swamps and other precautionary measures were conducted in both the Canal Zone and the republic proper and the diseases, as well as the insects, were virtually eliminated from the isthmus. In the end, the United States had tamed a jungle.

Seven sets of locks raise and lower ships twenty four hours a day to link them between the oceans. It takes approximately eight hours for a ship to transit the route. About fifty ships per day move through the canal. Major accidents are rare and in all the years of the canal's operation only four ships have sunk in the waterway, temporarily halting the passage of ships. Three artificial lakes provide the water for a controlled system that make the canal locks function.

The canal that brought Panama and the United States together also drove them apart. From the time construction began in 1904 until 1933, Panama was governed by the old elite, the fathers of independence. They disdained the poor and ethnic minorities, especially the West Indian blacks who came to the isthmus to help construct the canal. The Panamanian elite tried to keep politics among themselves and willingly identified with the North Americans. During this same time period, U. S. policymakers preferred political tranquility in Panama and when civil disruptions threatened, the United States helped to suppress them. On canal issues, the Panamanians were more concerned with a sense of shared sovereignty which, if it did not interfere with the canal's operation, maintenance and defense, U.S. policymakers were willing to negotiate. But neither appeared to understand the economic plight of the middle and lower sector groups. This was best seen in the violence that erupted in 1926 when the Panamanian people learned that a proposed new treaty provided them no benefits.

Two forces drove Panama's restless undercurrent. One was the middle sector, a generation of Panamanians removed from the independence movement who enjoyed the economic benefits of the country but were denied political privilege. From this sector came *Acción Comunal* that engineered a coup in 1931 that set in motion a conflict between them and the old upper class. The second faction was the labor force, which was divided into two groups: native Panamanians and the West Indians and their descendants. Although they shared common social ills, poor pay, unemployment and underemployment, neither group supported the other and, in fact, the Panamanians wished to expatriate the West Indians. The Panamanians found a leader in Arnulfo Arias, while the West Indians retreated into their own cultural conclaves and did not, until near the end of World War II, begin to organize their own labor groups. In this sea of constant strain and conflict, the military emerged as an important political factor. Colonel José Remón transformed the Panamanian police force into a potent weapon and he appeared to offer programs that satisfied both groups. In the midst of this tempest, the United States clung to its policy of retaining alleged sovereign control over the canal and the zone. Concurrently, the Panamanian middle and lower socio-economic groups came to understand that the informal alliance between the ruling elite and the United States officials did not benefit them. The 1936 and 1955 treaties and the violent demonstrations in 1959 and 1964 are testimony to that fact.

The constant political turmoil provided General Omar Torrijos the opportunity to seize power in 1968. From then until December 1989, the military became Panama's political arbiter. Torrijos introduced programs that reached down to those at the bottom of Panama's socio-economic scale, while at the same time he attempted to pacify the middle and upper classes. He capitalized upon Panama's nationalistic aspiration to own the canal and the belief that it would provide the economic where-with-all to address the nation's economic and social ills. Beginning in 1964, leadership in Washington accepted the notion that the canal could no longer be governed by the United States alone, since the changing pattern of world politics made ownership of the canal a defenseless issue. The end result was the 1977 treaties that provided for turning over the canal to Panama in the year 2000. While the Panamanians gave quick approval to the new treaties, the North Americans clung to the old issues of sovereignty and commercial and defense needs until 1979, when President Jimmy Carter, with his political life at stake, engineered the Senate's approval of the new treaties.

Rather than a new era in U.S.-Panamanian relations envisioned by Carter and Torrijos, the canal became the focal point of confrontation between Manuel Noriega in Panama City and Ronald Reagan and George Bush in Washington. Following Torrijos' death in 1981, Manuel Noriega emerged as a political tyrant. A sexual deviant who pursued religious ideas and practices not common in Panama, Noriega brutally suppressed his political opponents, engaged in drug trafficking and money laundering and served as a double agent between Fidel Castro in Cuba, the Sandinistas in Nicaragua and the Central Intelligence and the Drug Enforcement Agencies in Washington. He became so irritating to the Reagan administration that a decision was made to topple him by economic strangulation. When that failed, George Bush ordered an invasion of Panama in December 1989, which resulted in the apprehension of Noriega and his transport to Miami where he was finally convicted of a series of drug related crimes. The military's loss of political power in Panama meant a restoration of the old order. President Guillermo Endara represented the white commercial elite, thus re-igniting the political tension that has long characterized Panamanian politics. From Washington's perspective, that tension, with its economic and social disparities, threatens to affect the operation of the canal and has raised questions about the need to revise the 1977 treaties. Thus, in 1992, the United States and Panama have come full circle from where they had begun their relationship in 1903.

This volume differs from other monographs about Panama and the United States. Whereas the majority of the literature focuses solely upon Panama's political history or incorporates it into a history of United States-Panamanian relations, this volume treats each subject separately. It first analyzes the republic's political development, explaining the internal dynamics exclusive of the canal issue. The second chapter examines the history of United States relations with Panama regarding the canal, focusing upon the objectives that each nation had in its diplomatic dealings with the other. The third chapter brings Panama's political dynamics and the canal issue together during the recent regime of Manuel Noriega and relates that period to the historic past. The reader should also note that the first two chapters are sub-divided into roughly equal time periods, so that those wishing to correlate Panama's political dynamics with United States-Panamanian diplomatic relations can do so.

Many individuals assisted in the preparation of this volume, but space only permits the acknowledgement of a few. A special thanks to Richard Dean Burns, not only for the opportunity to undertake this project, but also for his assistance and patience in seeing it to its conclusion. As always, Bruce Latimer, at the University of North Florida's Thomas G. Carpenter Library, found the time to track down needed materials. Michael Mueller graciously helped with the preparation of the final manuscript. Yet, I remain responsible for any errors of fact.

Thomas M. Leonard
University of North Florida
Jacksonville, Florida

Chapter One

ELITES AND GENERALS: PANAMA'S POLITICAL HISTORY

For three centuries following Panama's discovery in 1513, conquerors, exploiters and tourists visited the isthmus, imbedding upon it traits that continue to characterize Panamanian politics into the contemporary period. The Spanish came first to be followed by European buccaneers, railroad and canal entrepreneurs and finally, North Americans. The foreign presence contributed to the concentration of Panamanian political power in the hands of a few, who in turn bloated government payrolls with their friends and families. Until 1968, Panamanian politics could be described as a tribal affair as public office passed between families of the oligarchy who had wealth, aristocratic background or both. From October 1968 to December 1989 the tribal politics remained, but instead of the civilian oligarchy, military officers became the politicians. In both instances the vast majority of Panamanians, mostly unskilled and poverty stricken, remained outside the political arena. The United States did not enter the political arena except when its interests in the transisthmian canal were threatened.

FROM A COLONY TO A NATION: 1513 TO 1903

In Panama ,as elsewhere in the New World, Spain established a centralized government. Initially, Panama was placed under the jurisdiction of the Viceroy of Peru, from which the appointed *gobernador* (governor) and *audencia* (court) implemented Spanish laws, oversaw trade and collected the king's share of the colonial wealth. Although Panama itself possessed little wealth, it served as the crossroad for Spanish trade. Panama became the distribution point for commerce with Central America and the west coast of South America,and with the Philippines, until Acapulco, Mexico received the monopoly on the East Asia route in 1600. The wealth that transited the isthmus also attracted European challengers and buccaneers, like Francis Drake and Henry Morgan. In the early seventeenth century, shifting European alliances and a decline in New World wealth markedly contributed to Europe's decreased interest in the isthmus. As a result of administrative reorganization in 1739, Spain transferred jurisdiction of Panama to the Viceroyalty of New Granada (Colombia). Thereafter, Panama became an isolated outpost barely capable of supporting itself. In this vacuum, Mosquito Indians from Nicaragua penetrated far south on Panama's Pacific coast.

As elsewhere in Spain's New World empire, the Roman Catholic Church held a privileged position within a rigid social structure. The extremely close church-state relationship permitted both the secular church and the religious orders to accumulate wealth, but owing to Panama's poverty, it never approached the sums found elsewhere in the New World empire. The church concentrated its efforts in Panama City, but lacking wealth and talented individuals, its influence declined by the time of Latin America's independence from Spain in the early nineteenth century.

More enduring was the rigid social structure that characterized colonial Panama. *Peninsulares* (persons born in Spain) occupied the top position of the social pyramid. They received government appointments, controlled commerce and enjoyed social privilege. *Criollos* (persons of pure Spanish blood born in the New World) held minor government posts, engaged in commerce and became rural landowners. Because the *criollos* did not enjoy the same political, economic and social status as their Iberian relatives, jealousy characterized their relationship. *Mestizos* (the offspring of a Spanish and Indian union) ranked below the two white groups but at times benefitted from the

Spanish connection. Indians and enslaved blacks occupied the lowest social ranking and were denied political and civil rights and the opportunity for social mobility. Panama's first census, taken in 1793, and which omitted most indians, rural dwellers, soldiers and priests, counted 71,888 inhabitants in the colony, 7,857 of them in Panama City. Several other towns ranged in size from 2,000 to 5,000 persons.

The first Spanish colonists founded towns and farmed the best land along the Pacific coast. These *interioranos* formed a rural oligarchy, which while not wealthy, controlled both land and people. As the port cities developed, their populations became more diverse: bureaucrats, military, merchants, seamen, artisans and black slaves. These *portenos*, particularly the *peninsulare* and *criollo* elites linked to the isthmian commerce, became more sophisticated and cosmopolitan than their rural counterparts. As the colonial period progressed, the divergent political and economic interests increasingly separated the *portenos* and *interioranos*.

Independence came to Panama without the violence that characterized most of Latin America's separation from Spain. Panamanians remained aloof from the early nineteenth century separatist movements, but the aloofness did not prevent revolutionaries from seeking to use the isthmus' strategic location for their own purposes. For example, General Francisco Miranda offered Great Britain a canal concession across the isthmus in return for aid to the revolutionary cause. Spanish patriots from Colombia attempted to take control of Portobelo in 1814 and again in 1819. Subsequently, a naval expedition from liberated Chile captured Taboga Island in the Bay of Panama. Independence came to the isthmian state in 1821 when the Spanish Viceroy at Bogotá deserted the liberated New Granada for Ecuador. He left behind as acting governor a native Panamanian, Colonel Edwin Fábrega, who succumbed to the growing pressure for separation from Spain. At Panama City on November 28, 1821, Panama declared its independence, after which the Panamanian elite debated the advantages and disadvantages of a relationship with Peru, Mexico or Gran

Colombia. The Panamanians agreed to become part of Simón Bolívar's Gran Colombia, a state that included the present day nations of Colombia, Ecuador and Venezuela.

The legacies of the colonial experience dominated Panama's nineteenth century political development. Throughout that century, the Panamanian-Colombian conflict overshadowed the department's internal urban-rural conflict. Initially, the Panamanians claimed that because of their voluntary affiliation with Colombia, their state remained an autonomous area with special trading privileges. Colombia's political leadership, however, never recognized Panama's claim to autonomy. Instead, their policies toward the isthmian state reflected the philosophy of the various governments that occupied the presidential palace at Bogotá. Liberals permitted a greater degree of local self government, including limitations on the privileged position of the church. In contrast, Conservatives favored a strong central government and church privileges. In Colombia, the constant political conflict between the Liberals and Conservatives throughout the nineteenth century resulted in the Panama Department having forty different administrations, fifty riots and rebellions, five attempted secessions and thirteen United States interventions under the provisions of the 1846 Bidlack-Mallinaro Treaty. The chaos often contributed to attempted coup d' etats by troops of the central government, by factions out of political power and by citizens opposed to governmental edicts. The violence culminated in 1885 with the destruction of Colón and the landing of United States forces there and at Panama City to protect the transisthmian railroad.

While the Panamanian-Colombian conflict received the most attention, the department's internal political dynamics were equally contentious. From the earliest days of Spanish occupation, Panama's interior offered little to attract colonization and those *criollos* who migrated there concentrated their efforts in the Pacific coastal area where they engaged in raising cattle for local consumption. By 1873 there were 4,512 cattle ranches dotting the Pacific coastal region. Most of these were small scale operations. Ninety-two percent of the cattlemen had herds of less than 100 head, which made them vulnerable to the urban entrepreneurs who controlled the internal transportation system and the slaughterhouses in Panama City. Furthermore, rich urban dwellers owned the largest rural landholdings and held key political positions in the interior. In the late nineteenth century, the introduction of bananas provided an opportunity for foreign investors to expand their influence in the interior at the expense of the rural native landowner.

In contrast to the economic and political poverty of the *interioranos*, the position of the *criollo* urban merchants became well established. By the time of Panama's independence from Spain in 1821, they prospered from their role in the transisthmian trade and from supplying local military garrisons. Their wealth permitted them to purchase properties in Panama City and subsequently Colón. Politically, they assumed many of the government offices vacated by the *peninsulares* after independence. Their wealth and influence increased as the isthmus became the focal point of United States inter-coastal trade beginning in the late 1840s with the California "Gold Rush." The boom reached its peak between 1856 and 1869 when the Panama railroad carried an estimated 400,000 passengers across the isthmus and provided the urban elite with management positions with the railroad. Although the prosperity came to an abrupt end with the completion of the United States transcontinental railroad in 1869, the elite experienced a new cycle of prosperity with the French Canal Company that attempted to construct a canal across the isthmus between 1879 and 1881.

Nineteenth century economic developments also impacted upon Panama's urban lower class, whose roots could be traced to African slaves brought by the Spanish to drive mule trains, construct fortifications and mine gold. Escaped slaves from elsewhere in the Spanish empire found a haven in Panama where they formed their own communities near the port cities. By the middle of the nineteenth century, the former black slaves (slavery was outlawed in all of Spanish America with independence) formed the core of Panama's urban population.

This group of blacks took on the characteristics of Spanish culture. However, when the Americans began construction of the transisthmian railroad in 1855, there was a limited number of urban laborers, a factor that prompted the importation of nearly 7,000 Europeans, Asians and Caribs with a large admixture of African heritage. Most notable were the Chinese who survived the ordeals of construction and remained in Panama to become small shopkeepers. Subsequently, the French Canal Company also imported unskilled labor, mostly from Jamaica. In both instances, the newer black arrivals did not adopt the Spanish culture, instead retaining their British and French Caribbean heritage. The political strains of this social structure would become apparent after Panama's independence from Colombia.

The new Colombian constitution of 1886 that established a unitary state and made all departments subservient to the central government singled out Panama for special mention as subject to the direct authority of the central government. Panamanian discontent was recognized by the United States consul in Panama City who reported that 75 percent of the Panamanians would revolt if they could obtain arms and be assured that the United States would not intervene against them. Panama's increasing dissatisfaction with Colombia came at a time of increasing United States interest in a transisthmian waterway.

The concept of an American owned canal developed during the Civil War (1861-1865) and intensified with the French effort from 1879 to 1881. The apparent culmination came with a congressional report in 1901, which recommended that a canal be constructed on the San Juan River bordering Nicaragua and Costa Rica. The dallying of the governments at Managua and San José and the Spooner Act approved by the U.S. Congress led President Theodore Roosevelt to negotiate directly with Colombia for the Panama site, but the Colombians wanted more than Roosevelt appeared willing to pay. In this fluid situation, Panama's long unhappiness with the government at Bogotá led the Panamanians to Washington. Panamanian feelings about the government in Bogotá reflected a larger issue of regional conflict that marred Colombia's political stability and contributed to the outbreak of the War of a Thousand Days (1899-1902) between the Conservatives and Liberals. Although the fortunes of war varied, supporters of the central government (Conservatives) secured Panama City and Colón and the rebels (Liberals) controlled the department's interior. Following the rebel defeat in Colombia proper in 1902, the Bogotá government persuaded the United States to intervene in Panama. An armistice was arranged upon the *USS Wisconsin* in the Bay of Panama.

After the Thousand Days War, the distance between Panama and Colombia widened. The former found the latter wanting only to extract wealth from the isthmus, not to develop it economically. For Panama's laissez faire and internationally orientated urban elite, the Colombians were too restrictive and narrow minded. In early 1903, José Augustín Arango, a land agent and attorney for the Panama Railroad Company, seized the issue and determined to find others who would support the cause of Panamanian independence. Arango gathered other like minded Panamanians, many of whom were functionaries of the Panama Railroad Company: Dr. Manuel Amador Guerrero, Carlos C. Arosemena, Nicanor A. de Obarrio, Ricardo Tómas Arias, Federico Boyd and Manuel Espinosa. They were joined by U.S. railroad administrators James S. Shaler, Herbert G. Prescott and James R. Beers. Together, these men became the driving force for Panama's independence from Colombia.

In mid-1903, Beers returned to Panama from a stateside vacation where he had learned from his superiors that the United States government might lend tacit support to the independence movement. Encouraged by Beers' report, the would be revolutionaries despatched Manuel Amador to the United States. In late August, he met with William Cromwell, whose New York law firm represented the New French Panama Canal Company in the United States. After a few encouraging meetings, the discussions were broken off when the Cuban born owner of the *Panama Star and Herald*, José Gabriel Duque, to whom Amador had confided the revolutionaries' plans, had informed the Colombians that unless the Hay-Herrán Treaty were signed the Panamanians would declare their independence. Not intimidated by the threat, the Colombians informed Cromwell that the Panama Railroad Company would lose all of its concessionary rights were there a revolt.

The movement might have died there had not Phillipe Bunau-Varilla entered the picture. Bunau-Varilla, who had served as chief engineer in the failed French project from 1879 to 1881, formed the New Panama Canal Company in 1893 for the purpose of recovering some profit for himself and the many French stockholders. He also contracted with Cromwell's law firm to represent his company's interests in the United States. When the Amador-Cromwell talks ended in 1903, Bunau-Varilla stepped into the vacuum. Based upon his conversations with Roosevelt and Secretary of State John Hay, Bunau-Varilla gave the Panamanians assurances of U.S. protection and recognition in their pursuit of independence. Convinced that Bunau-Varilla was an important ally, the Panamanian revolutionary leaders made him minister plenipotentiary of the nation awaiting birth.

At the same time Amador received encouragement from Cromwell, several of his wealthy compatriots in Panama lost their zeal for rebellion. They felt insecure with only words, not a written document, that guaranteed U.S. support. They also objected to Bunau-Varilla's insistence that the revolt be confined to the proposed zone area and that the remainder of Panama remain in Colombian hands. Emotionally they recoiled at the sight of the proposed national flag made by Bunau-Varilla's wife; it too closely resembled that of the United States!

Still, Bunau-Varilla and Amador continued to plot. In the United States, Bunau-Varilla received continued encouragement from members of the Roosevelt administration. In Panama, Amador persuaded Arango, Boyd and Tomás Arias to continue the plot. Fortunately for the revolutionaries, they found Colombian General Esteban Huertas, who had served in Panama since 1890. He had grown to admire the region and, when confronted with reassignment home, chose to join the revolution.

On November 3, 1903, the various forces favoring Panamanian independence came together. The presence of the *USS Nashville* in Colón Bay encouraged the revolutionaries to

act. Also in Colón, Panama Railroad Company administrator
James S. Shaler refused Colombian troops' access to the railway.
In Panama City, General Huertas prevented his fellow
Colombian officers from taking action. That evening, the
Panama City council declared the nation independent and sought
U.S. recognition. It came three days later, guaranteed by the
presence of U.S. warships off both coasts of Panama. Almost
simultaneously Bunau-Varilla, who had become Panama's
minister to the United States by agreement with Amador, set out
to negotiate a treaty before any Panamanians arrived in
Washington. He accomplished that objective with Secretary of
State John Hay just hours before Amador and Boyd arrived in
Washington. The Hay-Bunau Varilla Treaty guaranteed
Panama's independence from Colombia, but only after ensuring
the interests of the United States and the New Panama Canal
Company. Despite the treaty's unfavorable tenor, the
Panamanians, relying for their own safety on the presence of
U.S. warships and fearing that Colombia would make a new
offer to the United States, quickly ratified the treaty. In so doing,
they transferred the republic's dependence from Colombia to the
United States.

Panama's independence did not address the internal political
dynamics. Conflict between the urban elite and the rural
oligarchy remained, while the urban underclass emerged as a
potential challenge to both. The latter had secured political rights
in the 1886 Colombian constitution and found their expression in
the newly formed Negro Liberal Party with objectives markedly
differed from the traditional Conservative and Liberal parties.
Given less attention at the time was the fact that many of the
foreign entrepreneurs attracted to Panama by the railroad, canal
and banana endeavors had married into the families of the local
elite. Equally important, but not part of the political dynamics in
1903, were the Asian shopkeepers who laid the foundation of
Panama's middle sector.

THE DEMISE OF THE OLD ORDER: 1904-1931

Immediately after the November 1903 revolt, Arango, Boyd and Tomás Arias formed a ruling junta. It represented the traditional Conservative and Liberal political factions and the interests of the Panama Railroad. Conservatives dominated the constitutional assembly which, consistent with Spanish traditions, established a centralized government that included a unicameral legislature and empowered the president to appoint provincial governors and court justices. Most provocative was article 136. Modeled after the Platt Amendment that had been tacked on to Cuba's constitution, the article permitted the United States to intervene in Panama for the purpose of maintaining constitutional order. At the time, the Panamanian Liberals understood the article to mean that the Conservatives wanted to secure their own position. With its work done, the constitutional assembly elected revolutionary hero and Conservative Manuel Amador to a four year presidential term and converted itself into a national legislature.

Panama's Conservative-Liberal struggle did not parallel similar political competition elsewhere in Latin America, where the controversy was steeped in the Hispanic past. In Panama, personalities and family status were more important than political ideology. The mostly white Conservatives traced their prominence to the *interiorano* elite and their employment by the Panama Railroad Company. Their minority political position prompted their sponsorship of article 136 in the Constitution, which permitted U.S. intervention in order to maintain political order. The Conservatives initial political popularity, like that of the country's first president Manuel Amador, rested with their role in leading Panama to independence in 1903. This same background made the Conservatives more popular than the Liberals among U.S. policymakers. Some even charged that there existed a tacit agreement between them, given U.S. acquiescence during the fraudulent 1906 elections and again in 1910 when the U.S. chargé d'affaires Richard O. Marsh persuaded J.P. Mendoza not to take the presidency following Jose Domingo de Obaldía's death.

The Liberals drew their support from a greater cross segment of society, which effectively divided their party into several factions. One segment was the rural white and *mestizo* cattlemen of Hispanic origin and their more recent cousins who farmed around the terminal cities of Colón and Panama. They disdained the commercial elite and the growing urban working class. Belisario Porras best represented this group. A second Liberal faction consisted of the immigrant businessmen attracted to Panama first by the transisthmian railway and subsequently by the canal. The Chiari family came to be the name most associated with this faction. Finally, the urban working class, consisting mostly of hispanicized blacks and mulattos, was cultivated in the early days by Belisario Porras. The diversity of support groups made the Liberal party susceptible to compromise candidates and contributed to personalized politics. One was a *Porrasista* or *Chiarista*.

In the first generation after independence, the Conservative-Liberal struggle and the concomitant *personalismo* dominated Panamanian politics. For example, President Amador and General Huertas confronted each other when the president filled government posts with Conservative colleagues at the expense of Liberals. The Conservatives won this initial political conflict, but they eventually lost the political war. General Huertas' resignation provided Amador the opportunity to disband the army and replace it with a police force. Buoyed by this success, Amador next rejected suggestions of office sharing between the two parties, a decision he came to regret, because when the Liberals captured the 1904 municipal elections they made it impossible for the Conservative president to govern. The Conservative position became so tenuous that they needed fraud and the National Police to ensure their victory in the 1906 municipal and national legislative elections. The turbulence continued, and the United States capitalized upon article 136 of the Constitution to insure free suffrage and to supervise the 1908 presidential election. Recognizing his party's unpopularity, Conservative candidate Ricardo Arias withdrew from the contest, leaving Liberal candidate José Domingo de Obaldía unchallenged. Partisan politics came to a temporary halt in 1912 when Liberal Belisario Porras won the presidency in an uncontested election. Porras dominated Panamanian politics until 1924, completing the term of Ramón Valdes who died in office in 1918 and being reelected in 1920.

Despite the political feuding, both the Conservatives and Liberals can be credited with a number of accomplishments. The Conservatives consolidated independence, introduced a new constitution, codified laws and established a monetary system. Culturally, they had the National Theater constructed, founded the National Conservatory of Music and encouraged the arts. The Liberals, particularly Porras, can be credited with many accomplishments. He continued the codification of laws, improved tax collection, directed the construction of telegraph lines and schools and modernized Panama City. He inaugurated Panama's first university, initiated a teacher training college, established the national lottery and national press and founded the nation's first modern hospitals at Santo Tomás and Panama City. In addition to extending a railroad line into Chiriqui Province to stimulate the banana industry, the Porras administration implemented a road construction program into the interior.

By 1924, the Conservative-Liberal political labels were no longer applicable. For the most part the old Conservative leaders had died and the Liberals had divided into factions. The parties became the personal preserve of political leaders who formed shifting coalitions for the sole purpose of winning elections. This was demonstrated when, after the 1924 presidential election was won by Porras' choice Rodolfo Chiari, a wealthy sugar and cattle baron, Chiari blocked the Porras' re-election bid in 1928 with his protegé Florencio Harmodio Arosemena.

In practice, the political system was dominated by the small elite class who tried to limit access to their ranks. The victorious president appointed governors, who in turn appointed mayors. The National Assembly rarely influenced the executive officers with whom they theoretically shared authority. Members of the ruling party used their position to grant government favors in the form of sinecures, contracts, concessions and honorary titles. The elite could not prevent ambitious men from breaking into public life, but when they did, the elite tried to buy them off with advantageous marriages, business partnerships, money and the like. The symbol of the newcomers' acceptance was membership in Panama City's Union Club. At the local level, political leaders acted much like political bosses in the United States during the late nineteenth and early twentieth centuries. They dispensed money and jobs, solved problems and arranged government favors in return for votes. The local politico could always conjure up a demonstration, although he did not consult with his constituency on government policy issues.

The elite also benefitted from the canal operation. Zone officials reserved sixty middle management positions for prominent Panamanians. Other Panamanian businessmen took advantage of the opportunities generated by the Canal Zone. For example, they built rooming houses, stores, taverns and brothels in the terminal cities to service the thousands of West Indians brought to Panama during the canal's construction period. Some Panamanian businessmen became junior partners in North American utility, banking, transportation and industrial projects that were related to the canal's operation. World War I prompted canal purchasing agents to contract with Panamanian suppliers for staples consumed in the zone: coffee, cattle, sugar and rum.

Outside this closed circle, two groups of people were frustrated by the lack of opportunity. The largest group were the West Indians (Barbadians, Jamaicans, Martiniquans, etc.) who had settled in the country after completion of the canal project. About half lived within the zone and the remainder in the terminal cities of Colón and Panama. Despite their diversity, the Panamanians labeled all West Indians *chambos* and discriminated against them. In response, the West Indians established a protective subculture that included churches, schools and fraternal and labor groups. The West Indian separateness was most evident in 1920 when they joined their Panamanian counterparts to strike for higher wages and job security in the zone. After Porras broke the strike, the West

Indians were not invited to become part of the Labor Federation of Panama. Instead, they remained a group awaiting political cultivation.

The second and smaller of the two groups outside Panama's political arena was the urban middle sector, which itself was divided. Ethnic minorities—Chinese, Indians, Jews and northern Europeans—pursued their economic activities, largely in Panama City. The other middle sector group was composed of urban professionals—engineers, lawyers, medical personnel and bureaucrats—but it developed into a political force. Tied to the economy outside the Canal Zone, these professionals desired opportunities within the zone for native Panamanians, but not for the West Indians. This group stressed the need for traditional Panamanian values and culture, including the Spanish language, and placed responsibility in Washington for the imposition of West Indian culture upon Panama. On August 19, 1923, some of these urban professionals banded together in a secret society, *Acción Communal* or Community Action (AC). In conflict with the more modernistic ways stressed by the ruling elite, *Acción Communal* feared government reprisal and therefore remained a secret society for the remainder of the decade.

Panama's potential political powder keg was exacerbated by its backward economy. Immediately after independence, the government failed in its efforts to break traditional landowning patterns. On the eve of the Great Depression, only an estimated twenty percent of the rural lands were under cultivation, and seventy percent of the farmers squatted on small plots of inaccessible lands. Despite government efforts, the illiterate *campesinos* traditional mistrust of the elite prevented them from seeking land titles to their plots. They continued to use the slash and burn system of clearing lands and bartered for things that they could not produce themselves. The large landowners concentrated along the Pacific slope also resisted modernization as they were content with the sale of their cattle and other produce to the port cities. As a result, well into the 1920s, Panama remained a net importer of primary foodstuffs to meet the needs of its urban population.

Similarly, Panama's urban centers failed to prosper after independence. In 1903, Colón and Panama City were little more than backwaters of development. The native markets resembled those of other Latin American countries selling fresh fruits, vegetables and other staples. Over time, small shops and department stores appeared and, after the canal opened in 1914, luxury shops multiplied in hopes of capturing a share of the transit ship and tourist trade. The vast majority of these businesses were owned by Asians, Jews and Europeans. Panama's industrial base remained small. At the end of the 1920s, breweries and distilleries flourished, benefitting from the U.S. prohibition laws that were applied to the Canal Zone. Other industries included textiles, hats and shoes. Sugar refining and meat processing plants satisfied local needs.

North Americans did not escape blame for Panama's failure to develop economically. Before independence, the United Fruit Company (UFCO) had acquired 23,000 acres and built 73 miles of railroad track. When the canal opened in 1914, UFCO owned an estimated $8 million dollars of property used for the exportation of bananas. Panama received precious few benefits from this trade. North American entrepreneurs also built Panama City's streets, railways, electric power company and telephone system. The Panamanian government borrowed heavily from U.S. banks to pay for these infrastructure projects. On the eve of the Great Depression, North Americans had nearly $29 million in direct investments in Panama and held $18 million in Panamanian bonds. U.S. products accounted for nearly two thirds of Panamanian imports and the United States took in nearly ninety-five percent of the republic's exports. For the Panamanian business community, the most visible U.S. penetration of their economy was the canal's commissary operation. Established in 1905 in response to a critical supply problem, the commissary continually expanded its operations because the local economy could not meet the demands of the huge labor force imported during the canal's construction period. The commissary had blossomed from a pork and beans beginning to a silk stocking enterprise by 1930, monopolizing sales to Canal Zone laborers and their extended families and friends, U.S. government personnel and transiting ships and passengers. Not subject to Panamanian import duties and receiving favorable shipping rates from New York City, the commissaries stocked everything from food to fine English tableware and took on new enterprises, such as fuel and ship repair services. Local merchants were unable to compete on favorable terms.

Zone labor policies also impacted adversely upon the republic. Other than the few positions held by the elite, Panamanians were not eligible for administrative or technical jobs and were placed in lower paying jobs on the "silver roll," (wages were paid in silver coin) the same as the detested West Indian labor force. After the canal opened in 1914, traffic increased approximately fifteen percent each year until the depression, but the Panamanian economy and people failed to realize any of the prosperity. If anything, the local economy suffered from the continued decline in the zone's labor force, from a high of 43,000 in 1913 to 12,000 in 1929. The greatest number of those who lost their jobs were the unskilled laborers on the "silver roll," who were unable to find employment in the republic's underdeveloped economy.

Recognizing that they could not interfere with the U.S. construction, operation and maintenance of the canal, the Conservative and Liberal elite accepted the U.S. protective paternalism which set the limits on issues that the politicians could raise. The Panamanian elite also understood that the U.S. officials preferred to deal with the white upper class, in English, and that they preferred at least the facade of democratic and constitutional government.

The onset of the Great Depression in 1929 only intensified Panama's existing economic, political and social cross currents. As the economy worsened, so too did race relations. The government's inability to deal with these issues increased the level of political frustration. Finally on January 2, 1931 members of *Acción Communal* seized the presidential palace and ousted President Florencio Arosemena. The coup signalled a key turning point in Panamanian political history, as it brought to an end the generation of those politicians who had led the nation to independence and directed the formation of the national government and brought to power a new group of nationalistic political leaders.

THE POLITICS OF NATIONALISM: 1931 TO 1968

Following the January coup, Ricardo Alfaro served as interim president until the 1932 presidential election of Harmodio Arias. The son of nineteenth century immigrants to Costa Rica, Harmodio Arias belonged to the rural middle class. After studying law at Cambridge, England, Harmodio Arias returned to Panama and got caught up in the political dynamics of the 1920s. With the quiet support of *Acción Communal*, he was elected to the National Assembly in 1924, where he became the group's unofficial nationalist spokesman. Subsequently, Arias acquired the bilingual newspaper the *Panama-American* in which he spelled out his nationalist platform.

Harmodio Arias inherited a nation mired in economic collapse as a result of the world depression. With canal traffic drastically reduced, unemployment reached new heights, which in turn contributed to the rising call for the deportation of West Indian blacks. The economic collapse reduced government revenues and prompted Arias to suspend debt payments to the United States and appeal directly to President Franklin D. Roosevelt during a visit to Washington in 1933. Aside from economic issues, Harmodio Arias espoused the positivist philosophy that characterized *Acción Communal*. This neo-liberal philosophy, best described by José D. Moscote and José Daniel Crespo, called for a greater government role in society and an education program that stressed traditional Panamanian values and culture, including the Spanish language. In practice, Arias reached out to the poor with the *Fondo Obrero y Campesino* and the *Caja de Ahorro*. The former was a fund for Panamanian rural workers and farmers and the latter a savings bank for the urban poor. He also distributed some government lands to the rural poor. The establishment of the National University in 1935 insured the education of a new group of intellectuals trained in the neo-liberal philosophy which in succeeding generations increased the demand for government social programs, greater educational opportunities for the poor and limitations on property rights for the elite. Their nationalistic rhetoric also placed blame upon the United States and the West Indian blacks for Panama's lack of progress.

Because Harmodio Arias' failed to amend the constitution to insure his own re-election in 1936, he supported his Foreign Minister Juan Demóstenes Arosemena, who captured the presidency in elections marred by fraud and violence. Arosemena's presidency was of little significance except for the emergence of a new coalition political party, the *Partido Nacional Revolucionario* or National Revolutionary Party (PNR). The strongest faction in the coalition were the *Panameñistas*, who controlled Arosemena's cabinet and provincial appointments in order to prepare themselves for the 1940 presidential contest. The *Panameñistas* were led by Harmodio Arias' younger brother Arnulfo. He studied medicine at Harvard University, but was drawn to *Acción Communal* in 1930 and subsequently played a key role in the 1931 coup d' etat. Arnulfo served as Minister of Agriculture in his brother's cabinet and later as Minister to Germany and Italy.

In the 1940 presidential campaign, Harmodio provided the organizational skills to augment Arnulfo's charismatic campaign style. The *Panama-American* supported the PNR's candidate and platform, which emphasized "Panama for the Panamanians." Against apparent overwhelming odds, the leading opposition candidate Ricardo Alfaro withdrew from the race, but that did not prevent the elections from being obstructed by corruption and violence. Arnulfo Arias' reported margin of victory, 107,759 to 3,022, supported the victor's initial claim that he had garnered the support of the urban working class, the rural small landholders and cattlemen and the business community. But an impartial analysis concluded that Arias' support came from the day laborers and skilled workers of Panama City and Colón, whose economic livelihood was most threatened by the West Indian blacks.

Arnulfo Arias' inaugural address in October 1940 reflected *Acción Communal's* neo-liberal ideas which were even more clearly evident in the new constitution that Arias directed and implemented on January 2, 1941. The document's emphasis upon the state's social responsibility, nationalism and racial purity paralleled similar provisions that contained social policies in the 1917 constitution. It also reflected the nationalist characteristics of *Acción Communal*, in its limitations on foreign ownership of commerce, its guarantees for the employment of Panamanians in certain areas and a strict definition of citizenship. The principal targets of these provisions were the West Indians, Asians and Middle Easterners. Politically, the new constitution strengthened the president's hand by increasing his power over the legislature, extending the presidential term to six years and granting women the right to vote. Subsequently, Arias forced growers to sell their cattle, rice and sugar to the state and hinted at the nationalization of foreign owned enterprises in the republic. The government also established a social security program, a public savings bank, an agricultural bank and a central bank and enacted a land reform law. Beyond these economic and social issues, the administration's legislative program mandated that all school children wear uniforms, that only Spanish be spoken in public places, that bars be fined for playing too much foreign music, that newspapers be censored and that PNR dues be deducted from government workers' pay.

Arnulfo's actions infuriated various elements of Panamanian society. The traditional elite, frustrated by the loss of political power, were enraged by the costly social programs that potentially provided the PNR with a strong political base. The middle sector, which included many of the commercial establishments owned by foreign nationals and their descendents, joined forces with the traditionally isolated West Indians in opposing the racial provisions of the constitution and legislative measures. Such widespread opposition, as well as U.S. dissatisfaction with his intransigence in negotiations relating to impending World War II hostilities, led to Arias' ouster in October 1941, while he was visiting his mistress in Cuba. When he returned to Panama to reclaim the presidency, Arias was briefly imprisoned and subsequently exiled to Argentina for the remainder of World War II. With Arias out of the picture, Justice Minister Ricardo Adolfo de la Guardia declared himself president.

The ouster of Arnulfo, however, did not suppress Panamanian nationalism. The *Asociación de Commerciantes y Industrialistas* wanted to ensure the limitations on foreign ownership in the economy. There was a widespread call for diversification of the economy and for industrialization in order to reduce dependence on the canal. Also, labor emerged as a potent political force with the establishment of the *Federación Sindical de Trabajadores* (FST), which sought to protect workers from dislocations caused by the end of World War II. During the same time period, cultural leaders continued to push for *hispanidad* and students gained greater voice in educational policy through the *Federación de Estudiantes Panameños* (FEP). Despite their disparate interests, these groups shared with the elite the anticipation of a return to constitutional, democratic government after the war. Instead of a return to democracy, President de la Guardia suspended the constitution in December 1945, an action that led to his removal six months later.

During the next four years, the Panamanian presidency was a game of musical chairs among the nation's most prestigious families. De la Guardia was succeeded by Enrique A. Jiménez, Domingo Díaz Arosemena, Daniel Chanis, Jr., and Roberto Chiari before Arnulfo Arias returned to the presidency in 1949. Beneath this charade at the top, Panamanian politics was undergoing a structural change that was not reflected in the 1946 constitution, which restored the four year presidential term and banned all types of discrimination, but retained many of the progressive labor and social provisions of the 1940 document. More important than the facade of constitutional government was the emergence of the National Police as a political contender.

During the canal construction period, the Panamanian police force was an insignificant organization of approximately 1,100 men under the direction of a U.S. superintendent. Following a confrontation with zone police in 1913, it was left with parade rifles without firing bolts. But following the 1931 coup, the role of the Panamanian police force changed. President Harmodio Arias selected José Antonio Remón to lead the National Police in directions independent of U.S. supervision and to serve as guarantor of his presidency. At that time, Remón, who graduated from the Mexican Military Academy, was the only Panamanian with formal military academy training. Throughout the 1930s Remón continued to receive technical advice from the Canal Zone police, but he did not have to fear United States interference because of the noninterventionist provisions of President Franklin D. Roosevelt's Good Neighbor policy. After the 1940 election Remón imprinted his own style by recruiting like minded officers, establishing calvary and motorized units and implementing riot control training. Although it never numbered more than 2,000 men, the National Police took on a military character and by the mid-1940s was poised to become the arbiter of Panama's tumultuous politics. The opportunity came in 1948.

The 1948 presidential election pitted Arnulfo Arias against the official candidate Domingo Díaz Arosemena. The established elite attempted to overcome Arnulfo's popularity by using gangs and thugs, known as *pie de guerra*, to intimidate the opposition. In the midst of the campaign violence, only Remón's police prevented the National Assembly from ousting the sitting president, Enrique Jiménez. When the government controlled election board declared Díaz the winner, Remón's police suppressed the subsequent violence fueled by Arnulfo's *Panameñistas*. In the continued violence that followed Díaz's inauguration, Remón's police became increasingly repressive. In the wake of Díaz's death in July 1949, Remón became kingmaker. President Daniel Chanis found himself removed from office when he attempted to fire Remón. When the Supreme Court declared Remón's cousin Roberto Chiari ineligible for the presidency in November 1949, Remón turned to Arnulfo Arias only after the latter promised not to interfere with the National Police.

Arias' short lived administration, marred by nepotism and corruption, became a disaster. With no sons of his own, he rewarded his brother Harmodio's offspring with government positions and fellow *Panameñistas* with cash, contracts and protection for their gold and narcotic smuggling operations. Bank managers made forced loans on favorable terms. Political enemies were forced to sell their properties at below market value. With the economic downturn that followed World War II, public finances became increasingly unstable, and a U.S. government reorganization of the Canal Zone operation only increased unemployment in Panama. The political corruption and economic adversity exacerbated Panama's tense political climate. In response, Arias sought to strengthen his own hand. He threatened the West Indians with loss of citizenship and suggested that the National Assembly be dissolved and the 1941 constitution be reinstated. Amid increasing protests and demonstrations, the National Assembly impeached Arias in May 1951. When Arias refused to vacate the presidential palace, Remón's police stormed the building resulting in the death of nine persons and the wounding of countless others. Arnulfo Arias, stripped of his presidential sash, was jailed for allegedly killing a palace guard and then sent into exile. With the overthrow of Arias, the National Police, subsequently renamed the National Guard, began its long road of ascendancy in national politics that did not end until December 1989.

In accordance with the lines of constitutional succession, Alcibíades Arosemena replaced Arias, but he was entirely dependent upon Remón, who dictated appointments and government policy. Remón's tight grip on the president, however, did not cure Panama's recession plagued economy. Throughout 1951, strikes and demonstrations became weekly occurrences which provided the National Police with yet another stepping stone in its rise to political prominence.

Remón seized the moment. He resigned from the police force to become a presidential candidate in 1952. In preparation for the contest he forged a five party coalition to create the *Coalición Nacional Patriática* or National Patriotic Coalition (CPN). He also appealed directly to the West Indian electorate. With his wife Cecilia, Remón campaigned vigorously across Panama promising the restoration of internal order, economic development and an improvement of government services, particularly in the rural areas. Often compared to Argentina's Eva Perón, Cecilia Remón became known as the *la dama de la bondad* (lady bountiful) as she distributed kitchen and medical supplies throughout the countryside.

Despite his appeal to the populace, Remón was burdened with a record of police repression, torture of prisoners and graft. Remón, himself, had a financial stake in several businesses, including cattle, gasoline wholesaling, construction, the daily *La Nación* newspaper and narcotics. The public, however, dismissed Remón's liaison with corruption in favor of his promises to change the course of the republic's political path. Remón captured 64 percent of the popular vote against Roberto Chiari and other lesser known individuals.

Remón 's immediate family lived in poverty, but their roots reached back to the colonial administrative bureaucracy and subsequently they had been part of the Panamanian upper class that was periodically marginalized by the cyclical nature of the national economy. Remón's opposition to Arnulfo Arias illustrated his ties to the traditional Liberal elite through the Chiari family. Remón 's first cousin was Roberto Chiari, the leading opposition candidate in the 1952 presidential contest. Thus, it was no coincidence that the Liberal and Patriotic Coalition parties survived the 1953 law that required 45,000 signatures to be eligible for participation in national politics. Arnulfo Arias' *Panameñistas* were conspicuously absent.

Remón's policies reflected his background. His agricultural program did not benefit the subsistence farmer, but rather sought to replace him with agro-industrial enterprises through mechanization, extended credit, price supports and rural electrification. He introduced economic reforms to cut Panama's dependence upon the canal and traditional lines of commerce. A redefined tax system aimed to reduce the government deficit and social programs focused on health care and education, but without the emphasis upon Hispanics that characterized the Arias proposals.

As Remón sought to please the broad spectrum of Panamanian society, the concentration of political power in his hands became offensive to most. He took a hard line against organized labor, denying unions the right to strike. He outlawed radical groups, jailed communists, imposed a 'voluntary' censorship on the press and weakened the judiciary through political appointments and intimidation. He converted the National Police into a National Guard with paramilitary responsibilities and benefits, including increased U.S. military assistance and participation in joint maneuvers with neighboring countries. These changes created a quasi-dictatorship that bore many similarities to the regime of Nicaraguan strongman Anastasio Somoza.

Remón's assassination on January 2, 1955, has never been adequately explained, but his death ended the CPN's stronghold on national politics. Although the CPN succeeded in having Ernesto de la Guardia elected president in 1956, the Liberals won in 1960 (Roberto Chiari) and again in 1964 (Marcos Robles). The peaceful transfer of power by three successive presidents gave the appearance of political stability, particularly given Arnulfo Arias' banishment from political participation. The Liberals also sought to ensure that there would not be another Remón in the National Guard. They preferred someone in tune with their interests. They found such a person in the new commander, Bolívar Vallarino, whose family roots extended to the colonial elite and who, after attending the Peruvian Military Academy, married the daughter of a brewery owner and purchased stock in a number of Panamanian businesses.

Beneath the facade of political harmony, the rising expectations of Panama's lower socio-economic groups increased the pressure upon the government to address their problems. The issue was exacerbated by a burgeoning population which reached one million in 1960. De la Guardia's administration undertook an ambitious school construction program and sought the resettlement of thousands of families forced to leave the Canal Zone after the 1955 treaty with the United States. Chiari, bolstered by the Alliance for Progress, directed the construction of a modern hospital for the Social Security Administration, established a short wave radio system to reach out to the rural communities and inaugurated the Bridge of the Americas across the Canal Zone. Robles, who won the disputed 1964 election over Arnulfo Arias (whose political rights were restored in 1960 when his *Panameñistias* supported Chiari), continued Chiari's public works programs that included the completion of a highway to the Costa Rican border and a hydro-electric dam in Veraguas. Still, none of the Liberal presidents were able to attract sufficient foreign capital to diversify the economy and to provide jobs for the lower socio-economic groups. This tension was reflected in the 1958, 1964 and 1966 riots, which resulted in the deaths of several people and injuries to scores of others. While these riots focused upon the United States presence in the Canal Zone and reflected the belief that if Panama owned its most precious resource its social ills would be solved, Panama's oligarchy did not escape attention. During the 1964 presidential campaign, Arnulfo Arias placed responsibility for Panama's ills upon the oligarchy. Even the oligarchy turned upon the Liberal government when the Robles administration proposed a revision of the tax structure as an impetus to economic development. Such proposals were unheard of in a nation where the influential elite had managed to avoid all taxation. These cross currents of political tension played out in the 1968 presidential election and the subsequent events that led to the emergence of Omar Torrijos.

Panama's 1968 presidential election marked another turning point in the nation's political history, because it resulted in a military officer moving into the *casa presidencial*. Whereas elections until 1931 were contests among the elite and those after 1931 a contest among the second generation Panamanians, 1968 introduced a group of reformers whose programs appealed to the poor at the expense of the oligarchs: Arias, whose nationalistic appeals now included the West Indian laborers; David Samudio, whose tax proposals angered the oligarchs; and Antonio Gonzalez Revilla, a Christian Democrat, who idealistically sought reform through the constitutional process. Rather than focusing on issues, the campaign revolved around personalities and alleged corruption that included impeachment proceedings against President Robles. When National Guard Commander Bolívar Vallarino accepted the Election Board's declaration that Arias had won the presidency, a faint ray of hope appeared on Panama's political horizon. Possibly, the elitist Liberals would work with the populist.

But tumult soon returned as Arias acted to secure his own position. Arias first reached an agreement with Vallarino, who resigned from his military position to accept a civilian assignment. He was to be replaced by his deputy Manuel Pinilla Fábrega, but Arias reneged on the agreement and sought Fábrega's removal and the exile of many of the Guard's top officers to foreign posts. Arias misjudged the degree of camaraderie in the Guard's upper echelon, because his actions triggered a coup on October 11, 1968, just ten days after his inauguration. As before, he found refuge in the Canal Zone before leaving for the United States.

The junta that replaced Arias was headed by Fábrega. The officers recognized Panama's political powder keg and, in an effort to diffuse it, sought to placate both the oligarchs and the lower socio-economic groups. The junta's political appointees were individuals like Eduardo Morgan, who had links to the Chiari family, as Minister of Government and Justice; Henry Ford, former president of the Chamber of Commerce, as Minister of Finance; and Juan Materno Vásquez, a black activist lawyer, as Minister to the President.

While attention focused upon the make up of the junta, the National Guard experienced its own crisis. Vallarino's resignation had set off a competition for the Guard's leadership between Lieutenant Colonel Omar Torrijos Herrera and Major

Boris Martínez. By early December, Torrijos became commander-in-chief and Martínez chief of staff. Still, their personal rivalry continued. When Martínez announced an agrarian reform program and that the Guard would no longer quell public demonstrations, he angered the oligarchs and the zone officials. Isolated, Martínez found himself on a plane for the Inter-American Defense College in the United States. Torrijos was now alone at the top.

THE REGIME OF OMAR TORRIJOS: 1968-1980

Torrijos, born to middle sector parents in Veraguas Province in 1929, belonged to a generation of Panamanians that experienced neither independence nor the 1931 coup. He attended the Santiago Normal School, considered the most important center of student nationalism in Panama's interior. As a boy he often visited Panama City where he developed a distaste for the arrogant behavior of the U.S. military. After attending the Salvadoran Military Academy for five years, he returned to Panama in 1951 only to find himself outside the oligarchy circles. He came to despise the infamous Union Club, where the elite determined the fortune of Panamanian politics. Torrijos' small town demeanor only concealed his strong feelings.

In his effort to consolidate power, Torrijos brutally suppressed the opposition, utilized the Guard's Intelligence Unit (G-2) to identify his enemies, encouraged Guard officers to profit from their positions in government and promoted officers frequently. To gain popular support for the Guard he used civic action programs. His regime can be divided into three time periods. During the first, 1968 to 1972, Torrijos ruled through decree after abolishing political parties and stripping the National Assembly and presidency of authority. He sought to develop a mix of domestic and foreign policies that would secure his position. In the second period, 1972 to 1976, he institutionalized his previous actions. For example, article 277 of the 1972 constitution designated Torrijos as the "Maximum Leader" of the revolution and granted him extraordinary powers for six years that permitted him to appoint almost all government officials. An Assembly of *Corregimientos* replaced the defunct National Assembly. The new assembly consisted of 505 delegates elected from districts that could be traced to the colonial period. This act denied the business and commercial elites influence over government policy making. In the final phase, 1976-1980, the economy worsened as the process of import-substitution stagnated and the national debt markedly increased. The worsening economic crisis prompted a revision of the constitution in 1978, which took away many of Torrijos's powers and led to the appointment of Aristides Royas as civilian president, the establishment of the Democratic Revolutionary Party (PRD) and the scheduling of presidential elections for 1984. The characteristics of these time periods can be seen in Torrijos's policies toward Panama's various socio-political constituencies.

Immediately after seizing power, Torrijos had to deal with the commercial-industrial elites who historically had played a dominate role in Panamanian politics. Their wealth dated to the colonial days and remained in the hands of a few. For example, in 1960, 36 of the nation's largest 120 national companies were controlled by three families. This group controlled the Union Club, the National Council for Private Enterprise (CONEP) and the Liberal Party until its fractionalized division in the 1960s. Torrijos also catered to the so-called *tecnicos*, such as David Samudio. Because they supported his reform programs, Torrijos rewarded them with government posts and contracts. When the economy slowed in 1974, Torrijos established the Ministry of Commerce and Industry to insure the elite's input into the economic decision making process. But the economy continued to deteriorate causing popular protests and demonstrations to intensify. The crisis culminated in February 1976, when Torrijos met with members of CONEP who demanded a tripartite commission (composed of the Minister of Labor and business and union leaders) to reconcile their differences. The result was a revision to the Labor Code in December 1976, that effectively reduced wages, imposed new restrictions on unionization efforts and set limitations on the right to strike. Having won the initial victory, the business community continued to pressure Torrijos for a role in government and the restoration of political parties.

On the eve of Torrijos' coup, labor was poised to play a significant political role largely due to changes in the Panamanian economy since 1945. Until then, the national perception was that the vast majority of urban workers were "foreigners" tied to the Canal Zone and a smaller group of Panamanians employed in the nation itself. World War II disrupted the importation of manufactured goods into Panama and prompted the expansion of local industry, a process that was accelerated by the government's import-substitution policies of the 1950s and the opening of the Canal Zone market and increased wages for Canal Zone workers following the treaty revision of 1955. Although union activity depended upon the attitude of the political party in power, the number of unions grew from three in 1945 to sixty in 1965. During the 1960s alone, the number of workers in the manufacturing sector grew from 24,000 to 47,000. Hence, the historical perceptions of the labor force and its current fragmentation prevented Torrijos from creating one national labor union. In 1968, the most powerful labor union was the Confederation for Workers of the Republic of Panama (CTRP). Founded in 1956 as a reaction against the leftist drift of the labor movement, it maintained close ties with the United States American Federation of Labor-Congress of Industrial Workers (AFL-CIO) and the International Confederation of Free Trade Unions (ICFTU). Viewing the zone workers as "foreigners" who had identified more closely with radical ideology, the CTRP opposed Torrijos' attempt to bring them into a national union. Forced to compromise, Torrijos established the National Confederation of Panamanian Workers (CNTP) that subsequently became affiliated with the Communist World Federation of Trade Unions (WFTU). Importantly, the CNTP brought into the political arena those groups traditionally associated with the Canal Zone and rural agro-export orientated industries and made labor a potentially disruptive force. The slowdown in economic growth after 1974 forced Torrijos to amend the Labor Code in 1976 to slow the unionization process because labor's demands could not be met due to the weak economy.

In 1969, Torrijos conducted a serious campaign to expand his rural political base, where, with the exception of the black laborers in the banana zones, *mestizos* and indians worked as cattlemen and subsistence farmers. As cattle raising increased between 1950 and 1968, the amount of land available to peasants for subsistence farming markedly declined. As a result, peasants became increasingly dependent upon the cattle ranchers. To cut the dependency and build a political base, Torrijos instituted the *asentamientos* (cooperatives) land distribution program whereby the government purchased and sold to the peasants tax delinquent properties. By 1977 some 500,000 hectares of land had been obtained for the establishment of 372 *asentamientos* to the benefit of 12,532 families. In 1970 the government formed the National Confederation of *Asentamientos* (CONAC) which provided the peasantry with representation in government for the first time in Panamanian history. In 1972 twenty peasant leaders were elected to the Assembly of *Corregimientos*. Still, the efforts at cooperative farming were mixed. Peasants who previously rented lands from cattle growers were more successful than those who had traditionally owned land. As with the unionization efforts, the government lost interest in the rural workers when the economy slowed in 1974.

As elsewhere in Latin America during the 1970s, the migration of Panamanian rural dwellers to urban centers intensified. In 1950, 36 percent of Panama's population resided in urban centers. The proportion grew to forty eight percent in 1970 and 54 percent in 1980. The shift was prompted largely by labor displacement in the agro-industrial sector and by the belief that better job opportunities existed in the urban areas. While the urban poor traditionally resided close to the Canal Zone in low density barrios like El Chorillo, the more recent migrants congregated in more distant areas such as San Miguelito. The poor remained marginally employed, if at all. Torrijos aimed to improve their quality of life through building public housing projects and extending basic services, such as potable water and electricity to those without them. But as the migrants increased in numbers, Panama's disparity of wealth became more evident. For example, the average weekly wage for a Panamanian laborer employed in the zone was twice that of laborers in metropolitan Panama City. The wealthiest ten percent of Panama City's population received forty percent of income, while the poorest twenty percent received 2.3 percent.

Torrijos also restructured the National Guard and increased its role in the government policy making process. By the time of the 1968 coup, the Guard had become a highly professionalized and militarized institution thanks to the efforts of Colonel José Remón and to United States military assistance. It numbered 465 officers and 5,000 enlisted men. Torrijos maintained control over the Guard through a highly centralized chain of command. Eventually he approved all officer assignments, including the promotion of Lt. Colonel Manuel Noriega as head of the G-2 intelligence unit. By 1978, Torrijos had increased the size of the Guard to 700 officers and 8,000 enlisted men and shifted the location of their military schooling from El Salvador and Nicaragua to South America, particularly Peru. He stepped up the number of recruits from rural areas which effectively strengthened his ties to the countryside and he also accelerated promotions from the ranks that were mostly made up of the urban poor.

Prompted by the desire to forestall the potential of Cuban inspired communism, the Guard had come to play a significant role in public policy during the 1960s, a time when Torrijos was trained in civic-action programs at the School of the Americas in the Canal Zone. That experience taught him that social programs were a means to political security. Toward that end, the National School for Political Capacitation (ESCANAP) was established in 1974. There, officers and enlisted men were trained by cabinet members, labor leaders, politicians and other leaders in a wide range of economic and social issues. ESCANAP provided Torrijos with a cadre of supportive officers and with a mechanism to deal with the old line conservative officers who resisted his programs.

On the downside, the Guard was associated with the continued repression of the opposition, suppression of demonstrations and other violations of human and civil rights. Its participation in private sector businesses opened the door to increased charges of graft and corruption, particularly among the officer corps. In 1974, at the onset of economic stagnation, Torrijos increased public sector employment which provided Guard officers with another opportunity to increase their personal wealth.

With the exception of the Communist Party, the traditional political parties had no role in policy formulation during the Torrijos years. Panama's Communist Party was founded in 1930 and, except for the 1946-1948 period, had not been a significant political player. After it was outlawed in 1950, the party operated clandestinely as it sought to cooperate with those who had similar interests. Thus, at one time, they supported Arnulfo Arias and at another David Samudio. Torrijos agreed with the party's reformist ideas and even appointed some of its members to government posts. Although not recognized as a legal party until 1978, communists controlled the CNTP and CONAC organizations. They also had a central role in the Federation of Panamanian Students (FEP), the Panamanian Educators Front (FENAMUDE) and the National Committee for the Defense of Sovereignty and Peace (CONADESOPAZ). Their support was demonstrated by the election of sixty delegates to the Assembly of *Corregimientos*. The Assembly of *Corregimientos* had been designed by Torrijos to give the impression of broad based popular support, by giving equal representation to densely populated urban and sparsely populated rural subdistricts, each with one representative.

Despite the appearance of broad based support, Torrijos' popularity began to decline in the late 1970s. The fragile coalition of communists and gerrymandered districts opened the door to charges of incompetence against Torrijos and his general staff as the economy continued its downspin. With the 1977 canal treaties, Panamanians lost the anti-American issue as an explanation for their socio-economic plight. Despite the two-thirds popular approval of the treaties in October 1977, critics charged that Torrijos purposely limited information about the treaties and then asked for only a "yes" or "no" vote in a plebiscite the opposition claimed was fraudulent. Subsequently, these same critics stated that Torrijos knew in advance that the United States Senate would add restrictive amendments to the treaties once the Panamanians approved the documents. Against this backdrop, Torrijos determined that he and the Guard should withdraw from the daily administration of government, but not relinquish influence over it.

In October 1978, ten years after his coup d'etat, Torrijos "returned to the barracks." He relinquished his role as "Maximum Leader" and the concomitant powers granted to him in the 1972 constitution. He appointed Aristides Royo president and Ricardo del la Espriella vice president. Royo, a former education minister, represented the young reformists and Espriella, a banker, sent a positive signal to the business community.

At the time Torrijos "returned to the barracks" he also prepared for Panama's transition to democracy, beginning with the election of a National Legislative Council in 1980 and culminating with general elections in 1984. Toward that end, Torrijos permitted the return of political exiles, including Arnulfo Arias, and the reappearance of political parties. The parties, however, needed a verifiable count of 30,000 members before receiving official recognition, a move designed to prevent the proliferation of parties and the manipulation of smaller groups by larger ones. Torrijos clearly intended to establish a party that would represent the military, its interests and constituencies. Thus, it was no coincidence that the first party to qualify under the new set of rules was the Democratic Revolutionary Party (PRD) which included a potpourri of middle sector, rural and urban labor groups and the marginal elements that had been attracted to Torrijos by his previous programs. The party's formation prompted immediate speculation that Torrijos intended to control the 1980 legislative elections and that he intended to be a candidate in the 1984 presidential election.

Arnulfo Arias' *Panameñista* Party, the Liberals and Christian Democrats also met the registration requirements for the 1980 election. Arias, however, refused to participate in the election process, charging that it was only an effort to legitimize Torrijos' bankrupt regime. Instead, he favored reaching an agreement with other groups that would protect his party's position from extinction. The Liberals remained split between the *Charista* and Samudio factions. The middle sector Christian Democrats hoped to improve their position through the democratic process.

Subsequently, a coalition of parties, the *Frente Nacional de Oposición* (FRENO, the National Opposition Front) battled the PRD in the 1980 elections, Panama's first free elections in over a decade. The coalition represented Panama's political spectrum: the strongly nationalistic Authentic *Panameñista* party, the reform-minded Christian Democratic and Social Democratic parties, Independent Democratic Movement and the conservative Republican and Third Nationalist parties. Such disparate ideologies suggested a marriage of convenience that focused upon a call for the revision of the 1977 canal treaties on terms more favorable to Panama.

In elections judged by most observers to be free and fair, the PRD captured ten seats and the *Frente* 7 (the Liberals five and the Christian Democrats two). Torrijos proclaimed the election to be a vindication of his policies, but critics pointed to the forty percent absentee rate, the fact that only nineteen of the 57 seats were open to election (the remainder were Torrijos appointees) and the number of laws that restricted the opposition's ability to campaign. For example, laws were in place that prohibited and punished actions that damaged a person's reputation, public security and order. The right to peaceful assembly was severely restricted, and demonstrations could be halted if they interfered with traffic or violated the rights of a third party.

Torrijos also faced difficulties within the National Guard when he "returned to the barracks." The conservative officers who opposed Torrijos' social programs objected to his selection of Royo as president. The opposition officers also resented Torrijos' assistance to the Sandinistas in their drive to oust Anastasio Somoza in Nicaragua. To check the Conservatives, Torrijos retired Colónel Rodrigo García Ramírez and abolished his position. Several other Conservative officers were also retired or transferred. For the moment, these actions effectively re-established Torrijos' authority within the Guard and severed the link between the Conservative officers and their civilian counterparts.

After Torrijos stepped down as "Maximum Leader" in 1978, he became increasingly dispirited and withdrawn. He continually distanced himself from government and Guard matters. Whatever his intentions, they came to an abrupt end on July 31, 1981 when his plane crashed into the top of a mountain in western Panama. While it may truly have been an accident, every Panamanian has a theory. Some accused Manuel Noriega, others the oligarchy, the leftists, the disgruntled Conservative officers and even the CIA. For certain, thirteen years of uninterrupted one man rule came to an end.

While we will never know Panama's fate had Torrijos lived, he changed the face of Panamanian politics. His socio-economic and political programs reached out to those who had been abused by the oligarchs: canal laborers and those employed in agro-export industry. His social programs in health, education and public housing expanded the government payroll, making the public sector the nation's largest employer. The programs, however, were dependent upon government borrowing abroad, which resulted in Panama having the highest per capita debt in the western hemisphere in the late 1970s. Torrijos also turned the National Guard into a social institution with its civic action and service delivery programs. While the Guard became increasingly professionalized, it retained its police force responsibilities that defended the regime by means that included repression and violations of human and civil rights. An undetermined number of officers were involved in illegal activities such as arms smuggling, prostitution, liquor distribution and, later, drug smuggling and money laundering. Their investments in the private sector that brought them government contracts also gave them a stake in the political arena. With the establishment of the PRD, the Guard's interests were politically institutionalized.

In the end, Torrijos intensified the strained relations between Panama's key political sectors. The oligarchy wanted restoration of their position and power. The poor wished to maintain, if not improve, their standard of living. The National Guard wanted to insure its place in the nation's future.

AN EMBATTLED DICTATOR: MANUEL NORIEGA, 1981-1989

Because he had not designated a successor, Torrijos' death significantly impacted upon the future leadership of the National Guard and the democratization process. Despite persistent rumors since 1980 that Torrijos intended to elevate Colonel Florencio Flóres, the absence of a transition plan set off a period of jockeying among the officer corps. Within the Guard, Manuel Noriega ranked fourth behind Colonels Flóres, Rubén Darío Paredes and Armando Contreras. Behind Noriega was Torrijos' cousin Colónel Roberto Díaz Herrera. He was the most politically active with links to leftist leaders, particularly among the labor groups. As expected, immediately after Torrijos's death, Flóres, as chief of staff, took command, but he preferred sports to the intrigues of Panamanian politics which contributed to his preference for the company of lower ranking officers to his colleagues whom he viewed as circling sharks.

Given Flóres' weakness, conspiritorial talks surfaced early, but the Colonels were equally mistrustful of each other. In this ambience they reached an agreement on March 8, 1982. The *Secreto Plan Torrijos: Cronograma-Compromiso Historico de la Guardia Nacional* (Secret Plan Torrijos: The National Guard's Historic Compromise Timetable) provided that Paredes would serve as commander-in-chief from 1981 to 1983, after which he would resign and run for the presidency in 1984. In subsequent order would come Contreres (1985-1987), Noriega (1987-1989) and finally Díaz Herrera (1989-1991). Noriega held a favorable position because it made him head of the Guard at the time of Panama's first presidential election since 1968 and provided him the opportunity to resign in time to seek the presidency in 1989. The completely isolated Flóres was forced to resign in March 1982, to be replaced by his own chief of staff Rubén Darío Paredes.

Flóres' resignation did not necessarily mean that the *Secreto* would be carried out. Before 1982 ended, Manuel Noriega would become the Guard's chief of staff. At first the *Secreto* seemed to hold as Paredes was promoted to commandant and general and immediately led the officers in an attack upon President Aristides Royo for the deteriorating economy and allegedly permitting government officials to take millions of dollars from government coffers through graft. When labor unrest climaxed with a series of strikes in July 1982, the Colonels removed Royo and replaced him with Vice President Ricardo de la Espriella, who recognized his dependence upon the Guard. Immediately upon taking office, de la Espriellla proclaimed the Guard to be his political partner. In accordance with the *Secreto*, Contreras replaced Paredes as the Guard's chief of staff. The situation completely changed by December 1982 when Paredes forced Contreras' retirement and replaced him with Noriega and made Díaz Herrera deputy chief. Many analysts concluded that Noriega had orchestrated these events in order to gain control of the Guard.

Outside the Guard, a civilian commission was established in November 1982 to draft proposed amendments to the 1972 constitution that would return the country to democracy. Among the proposed amendments was a reduction in the presidential term from six to five years, the establishment of a second vice presidency, the direct election of national legislators and the prohibition from political participation by active Guard members. These amendments were approved by national referendum on April 24, 1983, but public optimism was tempered by the fact that the Guard remained the key political arbiter.

Confident that the *Secreto* still held, in August 1983, Paredes resigned from the Guard in order to meet the civilian status constitutional requirement to become the PRD's presidential candidate. Optimistic about his own future, Paredes failed to recognize that several Guard officers were furious over his acceptance of a civilian plan to reduce the size of the military and that they supported Noriega's intention to prevent any civilian president from taking office. Early in September, Noriega emerged as Panama's "king maker."

In addition to the Guard officers, Noriega gained the support of disparate groups to undercut Paredes. He successfully appealed to many leading businessmen who saw Paredes as a threat to their own interests. With Panamanian leftists he shared a letter from Fidel Castro in which the Cuban leader promised to sever relations with Panama should Paredes become president. After Noriega convinced de la Espriella that he could become a candidate if Paredes did not, the president purged his cabinet of Paredes supporters. Void of any support, Paredes withdrew his candidacy on September 6, 1983. It was now apparent that anyone seeking the presidency needed the Guard's endorsement and particularly that of Manuel Noriega.

Noriega was born in 1934, the illegitimate son of his father's maid. According to distant relatives, Noriega's father gave nothing more than a name to his son. At the age of 5, Noriega's mother died, leaving him to roam the streets in Panama City until he was taken in by a school teacher, Luisa Sanchez. Noriega graduated from the city's most prestigious public high school, *Instituto Nacional*, where he was more known for the publication of an underground pornographic newspaper than for his academic achievements. Lacking the funds to pursue higher education, Noriega wound up mixing drinks at the estate of a wealthy Panamanian family and working a brief stint as a medical supply delivery boy. An older half-brother, Luis Carlos, arranged a scholarship for Manuel to attend Peru's Chorrillos Military Academy. After graduation, Noriega returned home to join the National Guard as a sub-lieutenant, where he latched onto the rising star of Omar Torrijos. While Noriega loved to associate with the elite, particularly in Chiriqui Province, his womanizing, deviant sexual behavior and religious obsessions gained him more notoriety. Long described as an insecure loner, Noriega trusted none of his closest advisors, relying instead upon his half brother Luis Carlos until the latter's death in 1981—afterwhich Manuel became more insecure and his behavior more deviant.

When Noriega took control of the National Guard in August 1983, he promised its reorganization so that it would be prepared to defend the Panama Canal in accordance with the 1977 treaties while continuing its leadership role in the nation's internal development. Instead, Noriega secured his control of the Guard and its use for his own purposes. From his new position of power, in October 1983, Noriega persuaded the legislature to approve Law 20 that changed the Guard's name to the Panama Defense Forces (PDF), with Noriega remaining commander-in-chief. While the law empowered the president with final authority over the PDF, it did not empower him to remove any incumbent Guard officer. The law also placed the army, air force, navy, canal defense force, police, traffic department and immigration under the command of the PDF commander-in-chief. The law also granted the military the arbitrary power to close down the press and to arrest civilians if their actions were offensive. Effectively, the democratization process was dead and the PDF and, specifically Noriega, was in firm control.

As the 1984 presidential election approached, Noriega's power became apparent. First, he forced incumbent President Ricardo de la Espriella to resign in February and offered the PRD nomination to Fernando Manfredo, an ally of the late Torrijos. But when Manfredo wanted to run unopposed, placing him in a position to challenge the PDF, Noriega withdrew the offer and turned to Nicolás Ardito Barletta. Considered an ideal candidate, Barletta had worked for Torrijos and for the ratification of the 1977 canal treaties. He had earned a doctorate on economics at the University of Chicago while the current U.S. Secretary of State George Shultz taught there. It was hoped that Barletta, having come from the World Bank, might find help in the international financial community to deal with Panama's $4 billion debt. Politically, Barletta had been out of the country for six years and had no local base of operation. As Barletta's running mates, Noriega approved Eric Arturo Delvalle, a wealthy industrialist, and Roderick Esquivel, a prominent physician.

Confident that sufficient opposition existed to the current political chaos and that the procedures enacted from 1982 to 1984 for a free and fair election would vault him to the presidency, Arnulfo Arias came forward again to challenge the establishment. But when the voting count was halted on election night, May 6, 1984, rumors of fraud spread quickly. The Electoral Board finally declared Barletta, the candidate favored by the U.S. government, the winner by 1,713 votes, a number allegedly picked by pro-Noriega representative Yolanda Pulice.

As a "Chicago boy" (monetarist follower of economist Milton Friedman), Barletta favored a reduced government role in the economy. Immediately after his inauguration in October, he cut back on government spending, fired some 15,000 public employees, instituted a wage freeze, raised local taxes and reduced protective tariffs. In so doing, Barletta infuriated every political sector. The poor were pained by the loss of social services, labor unions protested the layoffs, wage freeze and increased taxes and the business community viewed the lower tariffs as a benefit only to foreign manufacturers.

Equally significant was the increasing criticism of the PDF for its violations of human rights, corruption, drug trafficking and money laundering. And, as head of the force, Noriega came under increasing criticism for failing to control the PDF and for his links to the Medellín drug cartel, arms sales to the contras and coziness with Fidel Castro. The PDF's brutality climaxed with the slaying of Hugo Spadafora in September 1985. Spadafora was a physician turned revolutionary who went off to fight with Edén Pastora in 1976 against Nicaraguan strongman Anastasio Somoza. There he learned of Noriega's external connections and use of the G2 at home to eliminate opposition. Fearing for his life, Spadafora moved to Costa Rica in 1982, but he continued to monitor Noriega's activities. In early September

1985, Spadafora returned to Panama intending to expose Noriega. When he crossed into Panama on September 13, he got no farther than Concepción where he was detained by the PDF. Two days later his decapitated body, sexually abused and brutally tortured, was found stuffed in a U.S. mail sack inside Costa Rica. Amid a crescendo of protest in Panama, Barletta directed Attorney General Manuel José Calvo to establish a special advisory commission to investigate Spadafora's death. Barletta had played his last card. On September 28, he was forced to "separate himself" from the government and Noriega placed Vice President Delvalle in the presidential palace.

Delvalle, an heir to a sugar fortune, initially appeared much more responsive than Barletta to the needs of the poor. Among his first official actions was the restoration of subsidized prices for milk, rice and petroleum. But confronted with the same budgetary and debt problems that hounded Barletta, Delvalle reinstituted his predecessor's austerity measures. Again, the poor were squeezed.

At the same time, the middle sector became increasingly critical of Noriega. This sector had expanded rapidly after 1968 with the growth of the government service sector. While it supported the takeover of the canal in the 1970s, it now openly questioned the military's ability to govern properly and increasingly questioned the legitimacy of Noriega's imposed presidents. The middle sector called for constitutional government and honest political officials.

Amidst the growing tensions, Noriega expanded the PDF by some 4,000 men to a total of 15,000 by 1986. Explaining the need to prepare for the canal's defense in the year 2,000, Noriega created two new combat battalions. He rewarded loyal officers with swift promotions. In 1985 Noriega expanded the PDF's political participation with the establishment of a personal general staff that contained economic, judicial, international and national security affairs sections. This staff coordinated the making and implementation of national policy.

But all was not well within the PDF. There were growing signs of discontent. As the officer corps grew and became more professionalized, the competition for and criticism over promotions intensified. Also, a number of officers resented Noriega's increased corruption, drug trafficking and repression. This conflict reached a highwater mark in May 1987 when Noriega dismissed chief of staff and cousin of Torrijos, Roberto Díaz Herrera.

Díaz Herrera did not take the dismissal lightly. He publicly charged Noriega with graft, corruption, drug trafficking, fixing the 1984 elections and Spadafora's execution. Public reaction was swift. Previous apolitical individuals now participated in protest demonstrations. The National Civilization Crusade (NCC) or *civilista* group brought together the middle sector—members of the Chamber of Commerce, doctors, lawyers, small businessmen—whose sole objective was the restoration of democracy. Their symbol became the white handkerchief that soon appeared at all public rallies. The Roman Catholic Church openly joined the fracas, by opening its churches to those who were denied the right to public assembly and to Díaz Herrera to speak out against Noriega. Former Presidents Royo and Barletta revealed that Noriega forced their resignations and, as could be expected, Arias protested that the 1984 election had been stolen from him. Anti-Noriega graffiti became commonplace throughout Panama City. An August 1987 Gallup Poll revealed that seventy-five percent of the population in Colón and Panama City wanted Noriega to resign.

Noriega refused to budge and instead took to the offensive. The repression increased with the protests, as specially trained forces known as "Dobermans" used clubs, tear gas and guns to disperse the crowds. Opposition newspapers and radio stations were closed. Noriega apparently convinced the Panamanian poor, those blacks and *mestizos* who had been historically marginalized, that the United States had formed an alliance with the commercial elite to suppress them. Noriega organized these people into the Coalition of Popular Organizations (COPP) to counter the NCC. Noriega appealed to Panamanian leftists by emphasizing his connections with Fidel Castro and by inviting Nicaraguan President Daniel Ortega to Panama for the ostensible purpose of organizing a regional peace conference. When Noriega charged Díaz Herrera with treason, a crime punishable by a fifteen year prison term, the latter chose exile over possible capture. Confident of his position, Noriega refused a compromise solution offered by longtime confidant José I. Blandón. By the end of 1987, Noriega stood alone, with only his inner circle of military officers and PRD party leaders supporting him.

In early 1988 Noriega survived two attempts to remove him from power. In February, President Eric Arturo Delvalle found himself dismissed for trying to force Noriega's resignation. In March, a group of PDF officers failed in a coup attempt, but their effort forced Noriega to reconstruct his inner circle with more loyal officers to counter the lack of support by PDF's General Staff. The outburst of public applause for the coup attempt indicated the depth of the opposition to Noriega. As Noriega's circle became smaller, he recruited individuals from the marginalized sectors to form a paramilitary group known as the "Dignity Battalions." Deeply loyal to Noriega, these "battalions" became increasingly brutal toward those who expressed their opposition to the dictator.

Given Noriega's apparent resilience, the opposition fragmented. The death of Arnulfo Arias in August 1988 denied the opposition a charismatic leader. The Church, which never had been strong in Panama, was unable to bring the opposition together. The failure of the United States to intervene proved demoralizing. Confronted with economic hard times and without leadership, the Panamanian people turned inward for personal survival and began to plan for the scheduled May 1989 presidential election.

An eight party pro-government Coalition for National Liberation (COLINA), dominated by PRD, nominated Carlos Duque for president. Duque owned the Transit S.A. company, long considered a front for military owned enterprises. His vice presidential running mates included Noriega's brother-in-law Ramon Siero and veteran diplomat Aquilino Boyd. The main opposition group, the Civil Opposition Democratic Alliance (ADOC), nominated for the presidency Guillermo Endara, an ally of Arnulfo Arias. His vice presidential running mates were Ricardo Arias Calderón, head of the Christian Democratic party, and Guillermo "Billy" Ford, head of the National Liberal Republican Movement. Noriega became the center of the violence plagued campaign. Duque promised to keep him as head of the PDF until the year 2000, when Panama is scheduled to take over the Panama Canal. Endara promised to fire Noriega if he would not resign. Election eve polls indicated that Endara held a two to one lead over Duque.

The May 7, 1989, election was one of the most widely supervised in Latin American history and, for Panama, the most fraud free in its tortured political history. Although the Catholic Church's exit poll indicated that Endara held a three to one margin, the Electoral Tribunal announced partial results on May 8 that indicated Duque was ahead by six percentage points. The most notable election observer was former U.S. President Jimmy Carter who recognized that fraudulent vote counting gave Duque the edge, and he sought to persuade the Counting Board to mend its ways. When persuasion failed, Carter used a press conference to denounce the Panamanian government for violating the people's rights.

Public outrage followed the May 10 Electoral Board's announcement that Duque won by a two to one majority. The outrage turned to violence after the world witnessed on television the brutal pipe beating of Endara and Ford by Noriega's "Dignity Battalions" while the police stood by. That evening, Noriega had the Electoral Tribunal void the elections because of alleged foreign intervention and lost tally sheets. At the same time, pro-government and opposition leaders failed to work out a peaceful compromise, because Noriega refused to leave politics or the PDF. Subsequently, the Organization of American States failed in its efforts to negotiate a settlement. Finally, on August 31, 1989, Noriega named former high school classmate, Francisco Rodríguez, as provisional president, created a new National Legislature and announced that he would consider holding another election in six months.

In the spring of 1989, Noriega had narrowed and tightened the circle around himself and, although isolated appeared secure. The civilian opposition proved incapable of removing him and while elements within the PDF officer corps were disenchanted with their commandant, they had not developed a plan of action.

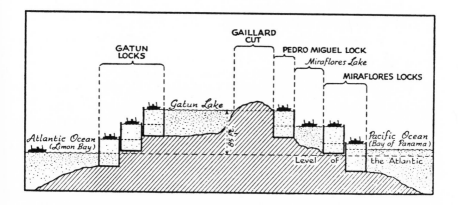

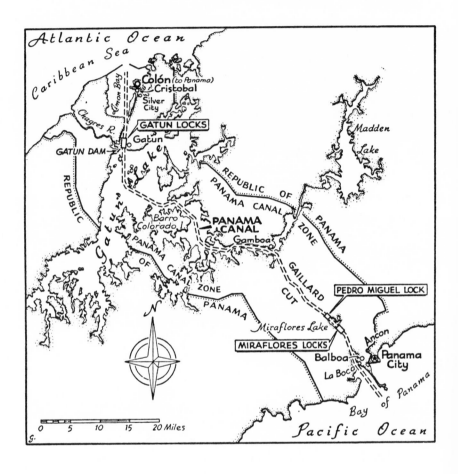

Chapter Two

SECURING THE CANAL:
THE UNITED STATES AND PANAMA

Until Ferdinand de Lesseps attempted to construct a transisthmian canal at Panama in 1879, the United States government envisioned an interoceanic waterway opened to world commerce and free of international political intrigue. Caught up in continental expansion, industrialization and a Civil War, the North Americans gave little attention to the project except to encourage private entrepreneurs.

That vision changed in the latter part of the nineteenth century as the European powers surveyed the world for colonial outposts, including an interoceanic canal. The de Lesseps project signalled a change in United States policy from idealism to practicality. Concerned with the possible presence of Europeans within striking distance of its shore lines, the United States pursued a policy that would secure the canal route for itself. That policy led to the U.S. intervention in Panama and construction of a canal there between 1904 and 1914.

The canal dictated United States relations with Panama. Always determined to insure the safety of the canal's defense and operation, the U.S consistently defended its sovereignty over the Canal Zone and hoped to placate the Panamanians with economic concessions. In dealing with Panama, the U.S. government preferred to deal with Panamanian leaders who understood and acquiesced to these objectives. Other Panamanians, such as Arnulfo Arias and Manuel Noriega, who had other agendas, were unacceptable to U.S. policymakers.

TO BUILD A CANAL: 1790 TO 1903

Prior to Colombia's independence from Spain, the United States had little contact with the isthmian state at Panama. During their own colonial period, the North Americans gave scant attention to the isthmus and from 1790 to 1820, U.S. trade was directed toward Europe, the Caribbean and Brazil, not the Central American isthmus. During this same time period, British resident merchants usually handled the scant U.S. merchandise that arrived at Panama, which itself had little to offer to the world markets.

As the Spanish American independence movements gained momentum in the 1810s, the call for United States recognition of the new republics increased. Among the leading spokesmen was Henry Clay, who envisioned a vast potential market among the former Spanish colonies. In 1822 the government in Washington ended its official neutrality policy and extended recognition to Colombia. In so doing, the United States indirectly recognized Panama, which at the time was a department of Colombia. Two years later, the Anderson-Gaul Treaty granted the United States most-favored-nation status with Colombia but the United States failed to capitalize upon the agreement. Instead, the British, who had financed much of Latin America's independence movement, gained the upper hand and effectively limited U.S. trade with Colombia during the first half of the nineteenth century. In fact, from the 1820s until the late 1840s, the United States demonstrated little interest in the events on the entire Central American isthmus. Trade with the region languished because of a general depression, lack of isthmian Caribbean port facilities, the more aggressive British efforts and the region's continued political turmoil.

While the North Americans seemed aloof to the isthmus, the Europeans, influenced by Alexander von Humboldt's *Political Essay on the Kingdom of New Spain* (London, 1811), expressed an interest in a transisthmian transportation route. Von Humboldt suggested nine potential canal sites, three of which lay in Panama. In 1830, a Dutch effort was aborted by the revolution in Holland. Next, a French company initiated plans. In 1835, a

Guatemalan, Juan Galindo, arrived in Washington with canal proposals in response to British expansion in present day Belize. Each of these projects were the vistas of private entrepreneurs. No one considered a government role in such undertakings. Similar thinking was reflected in 1835 with the U.S. Senate resolution that proclaimed any transisthmian canal should be open equally to all nations and that tolls be levied to reimburse the private capitalists who constructed it. Such machinations prompted President Andrew Jackson to dispatch Charles Biddle to the isthmus to make a detailed analysis of the various transisthmian projects and potential sites. In Panama, Biddle determined that the anticipated costs prohibited the construction of a canal there for several generations. In Bogotá, he negotiated a private contract for an interoceanic link via ship and road. Biddle's actions frustrated Jackson and the issue was put to rest for over a decade. As North American interests waned, the British filled the void, extending their influence along the ill-defined Mosquito Coast as far south as the San Juan River on the Nicaraguan-Costa Rican border, the long favored site for a transisthmian connection. When the North Americans rekindled their isthmian interests in the mid-1840s they found the British well entrenched in the region.

With the Treaty of Guadalupe-Hidalgo that officially ended the Mexican War in 1848 and the discovery of gold in newly acquired California, a new surge of expansionism gripped the United States. Many expansionists looked at the Central American isthmus as a means to transport people, supplies and mail between the east and west coasts. President James K. Polk bolstered the expansionists when he reasserted the Monroe Doctrine in 1848 to check European expansion in the New World. At the time, he directed his message against the British designs on Mexico's Yucatán Peninsula, but subsequently, he would apply the Doctrine to the isthmus.

A combination of this ambience in the United States and a change in Colombian political leadership resulted in the negotiation of the 1846 Bidlack-Mallarino Treaty (popularly known as the Bidlack Treaty). The treaty provided for the unrestricted transit of U.S. passengers and cargo across the isthmus by whatever means possible, provided the United States guaranteed the route's neutrality and Colombia's sovereignty over its Panamanian province. When Polk learned that the Treaty of Guadalupe-Hidalgo did not contain provisions for a transit route at the isthmus of Tehuantepec in Mexico, he submitted the Bidlack Treaty to the Senate, which ratified it in June 1848. The governments in London and Washington understood the Bidlack-Mallarino Treaty was a means to check the British, who were now looking beyond the San Juan River to Panama's Boco del Toro region. The stage was set for an American-British confrontation.

The tension intensified in 1849 when President-elect Zachary Taylor instructed his Secretary of State John M. Clayton to protest the British claims on the Central American isthmus. Special emissaries Elijah Hise (previously sent by Polk) and Ephraim George Squier (dispatched by Taylor) returned from Central America with Nicaraguan treaties that were designed to check the British on the Mosquito Coast. Not intimidated by Washington's emissaries, the British representative in Central America, Frederick Chatfield, ordered the seizure of Tigre Island in the Gulf of Fonseca, long considered essential to the operation of a Nicaraguan canal. Fortunately, cooler heads prevailed in Washington and London. Clayton understood that if the U.S. held a monopoly on any transisthmian route it would cause greater problems for the United States than Gibraltar had caused the British and the Spanish. He preferred an agreement that validated Henry Clay's instructions to the North American representatives to the 1826 Panama Congress and the 1835 and 1839 House resolutions, all of which disavowed any U.S. monopoly over a canal in favor of a waterway opened impartially to the world's commerce. In London, Lord Palmerston was preoccupied with the Turkish crisis, a surge of German nationalism and the perennial Irish problem. He too, wanted compromise.

The resultant 1850 Clayton-Bulwer Treaty pledged each government not to "assume any dominion over...any part of

Central America." For the moment, the ambiguous phraseology led the Colombians, the Central Americans and the North Americans to naively believe that the British had surrendered their claim to the Mosquito Coast and designs on Panama and that the benefits of the proposed canal would accrue to all nations. In reality, the treaty only prevented Washington and London from undertaking a canal project or fortifying it by themselves. Importantly, however, the United States had confirmed its strategic interests in the region.

While the United States was staking out its canal policy, technological developments in the first half of the nineteenth century led to new means of transportation and communication including canals, railroads, telegraphy, international cables, macadamized roads, streetcars and steamships. By the mid-1840s, British entrepreneurs were moving mail and passengers to Central and South America. Not to be outdone, the U.S. Congress, in 1847, approved legislation providing for the subsidization of a steamship line to link the east coast with the Oregon Territory via Panama. Within a year, several businessmen took advantage of the legislation to construct ships and charter steamship companies.

The California Gold Rush, that began immediately after the end of the Mexican War in 1848, inundated Panama with people and cargo that shifted Panama's trade from a European-West Coast of South America orientation to a United States East Coast-West Coast orientation. The magnitude of the shift in emphasis attracted immigrants and internal migrants to Panama's terminal cities and, in so doing, created the basis for future U.S.-Panamanian relations.

One of the entrepreneurs who capitalized upon the 1847 steamship legislation was William Aspinwall. He spearheaded a firm, incorporated in New York as the Panama Railroad Company, that took over a lapsed French railroad contract in Panama and reached an agreement with Bogotá in 1850 which set a precedent for future transisthmian projects. The agreement granted the company a 49 year exclusive concession to build and operate a railroad, plus all public lands needed for the railroad's operation and an additional 250,000 acres anywhere on the isthmus free of charge. Furthermore, the railroad's terminal cities were freed from Colombian trade restrictions and the railroad, alone, could set all tolls. In return, the Colombian government was to receive 3 percent of the company's dividends. Effectively, Aspinwall received the right to build and operate the railroad without government interference.

After spending an estimated $8 million in construction, bringing some 5,000 West Indian, African, European, North American and Chinese workers to the isthmus (an estimated 2,000 died on the job), Aspinwall's railroad opened in 1855. It soon assumed control of life in the terminal cities of Colón and Panama where the dollar replaced the peso and English replaced Spanish. Free of competition and charging exorbitant rates, the Panama Railroad Company prospered on its near monopoly of inter-U.S. coastal trade until the opening of the transcontinental railroad in 1869.

The department of Panama received little from the transisthmian railroad. The railroad did not bring the prosperity that was previously anticipated. Only the landowning elite profited from the exorbitant rents they charged the imported foreign workers. When the construction period ended, most of these workers lost their jobs, further weakening the Panamanian economy, a situation which worsened after the opening of the U.S. transcontinental railroad. The Panama Railroad Company bought up most of the land in the terminal cities, in turn selling or leasing it to foreigners for their railroad related enterprises. The Panamanians were also embittered by the alleged U.S. violation of the Clayton-Bulwer Treaty in expanding its interests on the isthmus and the refusal to permit British and French participation in the railroad's administration. The Panamanians viewed the North Americans as arrogant and condescending in their attitude and resented the interference of railroad police in their internal affairs, best illustrated in the so-called "Watermelon War" in 1856 that cost fifteen North American and two Panamanian lives, destroyed North American businesses in Panama City and damaged railroad property extensively. The

Panama Railroad Company set a pattern for future United States-Panamanian relations.

The United States Civil War, the Reconstruction period that followed and the subsequent urbanization, industrialization and westward expansion diverted U.S. attention from the isthmus from the 1860s to the mid 1890s. Canal advocates continued their call for a waterway under U.S. control, but the other issues denied them an audience. However, determined that a canal would increase the nation's prosperity and security, President Ulysses S. Grant declared the Clayton-Bulwer Treaty void. He also established the Interoceanic Canal Commission to study the entire canal issue. When it reported in 1876, the Commission recommended the San Juan River site over Panama because of its shorter distance and cheaper construction costs.

When Ferdinand de Lesseps undertook the canal project at Panama in 1879, he demonstrated the failure of either the 1846 Bidlack-Mallarino or 1850 Clayton-Bulwer treaties to keep other nations from undertaking a canal project through Panama. The de Lesseps project also prompted President Rutherford B. Hayes to declare before Congress in 1880, that henceforth it would be U.S. policy to build and operate a tranisthmian canal alone. Writing in *The Nation* in 1880, John Kasson warned that if de Lesseps completed his project, the Caribbean Sea would be converted into an American Mediterranean, a reference to the continued European conflict in that body of water. Successive secretaries of state—William M. Evarts, James G. Blaine and Frederick T. Frelinghuysen—called for a U.S. owned canal and the abrogation of the Clayton-Bulwer Treaty.

Meanwhile, de Lesseps continued to plod along. During the eight years of his project, a new wave of West Indian labor arrived at Panama along with thousands of other foreigners. As had their predecessors in the 1850s, the new arrivals found only the most menial jobs. When the de Lesseps project failed in 1889, some 13,000 West Indian laborers were left to form their own society in Panama, because they were never accepted by the Panamanians. As with the transisthmian railroad, only a few of the Panamanian elite found managerial jobs with the French, but many benefitted from real estate deals in the terminal cities. Importantly, the French canal administrators and the Panamanian elite shared some cultural traits and a common distaste for the Liberal party which appealed to the lower socio-economic groups. When this social-racial tension erupted into violence in 1885, the United States interference was on the side of the elite-white Conservatives, a preference that continued into the future.

The failure of the de Lesseps project pained the Panamanian elite who anticipated great benefits from the international waterway. They increasingly blamed the government at Bogotá for not contributing more to the project. The sentiment toward independence was building. As the mood changed in Panama, there was an opinion swing in the United States. The final private effort to construct a transisthmian canal began in 1887 when the Maritime Canal Company, formed by a former U.S. Navy civil engineer A. G. Menocal, commenced construction along the San Juan River. Three years and $4 million later the project collapsed, the victim of under funding, corruption and Nicaragua's political turmoil. By that time, however, the pressure for a government owned canal had reached new heights.

A coterie of imperialists, among them Assistant Secretary of the Navy Theodore Roosevelt, Admiral Alfred T. Mahan and Senators Henry Cabot Lodge, Sr. and Cushman Davis advocated a "large policy" to put the United States on even terms with the great powers and make it the indisputable dominant force in the western hemisphere. This included ownership of an isthmian canal. These men received a sympathetic ear from the business community. Chambers of Commerce, Boards of Trade and, in some cases, state legislative resolutions from California to New York to South Carolina and Louisiana endorsed a transisthmian canal in order to enhance the capability of the United States to expand markets in Asia and on the West Coast of Latin America. In addition to the material factors, leaders promoted the idea of a U.S. obligation to uplift what were seen as the world's inferior people. Social Darwinism became the explanation for the magnificence of the United States agricultural and industrial abundance, and expansionist advocates used it to justify the need to take western culture to the so-called backward areas of the world.

What began as a desire to prevent Europeans from building and operating a canal became a national obsession for security and markets and a moral crusade. By the century's end these forces converged to create a national demand for an isthmian canal built, owned and operated by the United States government. President William McKinley summarized this attitude in 1898 when he told congress that "our national policy now more imperatively than ever calls for its [transisthmian canal] control by this government."

Only the 1850 Clayton-Bulwer Treaty stood in the way, an agreement that both the State Department and the British Foreign Office understood had outlived its usefulness. The North Americans argued for its abrogation in order to build their own canal, while the British, confronting new political alignments on the European continent and the Boer War in Africa, were anxious for United States friendship. The result was a convention signed in February 1900, by the British Ambassador Julian Pauncefote and Secretary of State John Hay, calling for the complete neutrality and demilitarization of any U.S. built canal. The U.S. Senate refused the neutrality and demilitarization clauses on the grounds that an unfortified canal would not serve the nation's strategic interests. There, matters rested until Roosevelt ascended to the presidency in 1901. He instructed Secretary Hay to again approach the British, who this time proved to be more willing negotiators. The second Hay-Pauncefote Treaty permitted the United States to defend the canal.

During the period of U.S.-British diplomatic maneuvering, the question of the canal's location drew much attention. Public sentiment long favored the Nicaraguan route. So too did Secretary Hay and the Walker Commission, a group of engineers appointed by McKinley which issued reports in 1899 and 1901, recommending the Nicaraguan route at an estimated cost of $189 million, compared to $144 million in construction costs, plus an additional $149 million for the French Company rights in

Panama. Hay proceeded to sign protocols with the Costa Rican and Nicaraguan governments in December 1900 providing for negotiation of a canal treaty once the U.S. Congress gave its approval. Hay's plan received encouragement in early 1902, when the House of Representatives went on record favoring the Nicaraguan site with its approval of the Hepburn bill.

The immediate loser to the U.S. machinations appeared to be the New French Panama Canal Company, successor to the defunct de Lesseps organization. The new French company obtained from Colombia the rights to the Panama Railroad and an extension until 1910 to complete the canal. The French company benefitted handsomely from the operation of the Panama Railroad, but by 1898 had become discouraged with the seemingly endless costs of the canal project. Its asking price of $149 million was too steep for the North Americans, but in response to the Walker Commission recommendations, it lowered the price to $40 million in order to be competative with the costs for the Nicaraguan site. Prompted by the French company's change of heart, in January 1902 the Walker Commission issued a third report, this time favoring the Panama route because it offered better harbors, a shorter distance across the isthmus, the advantage of the already completed French excavations and less seismic activity. This prompted Senator John C. Spooner to propose that the president approach Colombia about the Panama rights. Teddy Roosevelt also seized the moment. Anxious to get the project started before seeking re-election in 1904, he declared for the Panama route.

Amidst these public declarations William N. Cromwell and Phillipe Bunua-Varilla engaged in behind the scenes lobbying. After 1898, Cromwell, a legal counsel for the New French Canal Company, did everything he could to sell the idea to the United States government that it scrap the Nicaraguan project and build a canal at Panama. Bunau-Varilla, himself an investor in the New French Panama Canal Company and its legal representative in the United States, conducted an unofficial campaign to sway the North American public in favor of the Panama site.

The stage was now set for a great debate, which began in the Senate in June 1902. John Tyler Morgan of Alabama, considered the most knowledgeable student of isthmian geography, appeared to stand alone in favor of the Nicaraguan route. Mark Hanna, from Ohio, led the cause for Panama. The controversy focused on the physical advantages and cost of each and the cost of acquiring the French properties. Only occasionally did isthmian politics enter the debate. In the end, the Spooner amendment to the Hepburn bill received narrow approval. It authorized the president to seek the Panama route first and, only if unsuccessful, to turn to Nicaragua.

In accordance with the Spooner amendment, Hay completed a proposed treaty with his Colombian counterpart, Tomás Herrán in January 1903. The treaty granted the United States the right to build a canal in a six mile wide zone across Panama in return for a $10 million cash payment and an annual subsidy of $250,000. In August of that year, the Colombian Senate rejected the Hay-Herrán Treaty, but instructed Herrán to continue negotiations in hopes of wringing greater financial concessions from the United States. If the French were to receive $40 million, the Colombians wanted more for their resource. After all, the Panama Railroad brought little financial benefit and the legislators wondered if the canal would be any different. Furthermore, the Colombians wanted their sovereign rights in the zone more adequately defined.

The Colombian position infuriated President Roosevelt. He refused to consider amendments, nor would he consider the Nicaraguan route. Although Roosevelt may have wanted an independent Panama, he could not openly encourage it because he was bound by the 1846 Bidlack Treaty that pledged the United States to uphold Colombia's sovereignty over Panama.

The Panamanians felt equally frustrated. By 1903 both the Liberals and Conservatives viewed Colombia's actions as detrimental to the local economy. They feared that the United States would turn to the Nicaraguan route. Independence became the common bond of the political rivals. They selected an elder statesman, Manuel Amador Guerrero, to assume the movement's leadership. In August 1903, he sailed for New York where he met with Cromwell and Bunau-Varilla. The latter also met with Hay and Roosevelt, who left the Frenchman with the distinct impression that the United States would recognize and protect Panama's independence. At the Waldorf-Astoria Hotel, Bunau-Varilla persuaded Amador of this, and with him, set in motion plans for revolution. Amador returned to the isthmus, where, with the assistance of the railroad's managers, 500 "bought" Colombian troops and the local fire department, he implemented the plan on November 3, 1903.

The day before the revolt, the *USS Nashville* arrived at Colón to prevent the transit of Colombian troops, thus ensuring the success of the rebellion. On November 4, other U.S. naval ships arrived to protect the independence of the fledgling republic. On November 6, Roosevelt extended *de facto* recognition to Panama. Taken together, these events lend credence to the argument that Roosevelt participated in the revolt's planning and was correct when he later proclaimed that he "took Panama."

When the revolt occurred, the Colombians sought an accommodation with the United States. Although Washington resisted the advances, Bunau-Varilla informed Panamanians otherwise in order to insure the completion of a treaty that would guarantee the republic's independence and, of course, protect the interests of the New French Panama Canal Company. The subsequent Hay-Bunau-Varilla treaty was written by the North American and slightly modified by the Frenchman. At no time during these discussions were Panama's interests represented. When the Panamanian delegation arrived in Washington on November 18, they were presented with a treaty that gave away their most precious resource. Reluctantly, the Panamanians signed the proposed treaty. Bunau-Varilla wasted no time. By cable, he warned Panamanian officials at home that if they did not accept the treaty, the United States would withdraw its protection of the new republic and again deal with Colombia. His argument was convincing. The Panamanian legislature approved the Hay-Bunau-Varilla Treaty on December 2, 1903. The United States Senate followed in February 1904.

The *Panama Star and Herald* correctly asserted that the treaty granted the United States everything it wanted, and that in return Panama received little more than its independence. For a $10 million cash payment and a $250,000 annual annuity, the Panamanians granted the United States the right to construct its canal. By the terms of the treaty Panama conveyed to the United States two sets of rights relating to the construction, operation and protection of the canal: (1) the rights of protection and intervention by the United States in Panama and (2) the rights of the United States in the Canal Zone.

Regarding the first category, North American rights in Panama were based in articles 1 and 7. According to article 1, "The United States guarantees and will maintain the independence of the Republic of Panama." Article 7 provided that the cities of Panama and Colón conform with U.S. sanitary regulations and that the United States had the right to enforce the standards. The same article granted the U.S. authority for the maintenance of public order in those cities and adjacent harbors and territories, if Panama, in the North American judgement, was unable to maintain such order.

The second category of rights-those within the zone-have caused more serious and lasting resentment in Panama. Articles 2 and 3 granted the United States wide powers for the construction, maintenance, operation, sanitation and protection of the canal. Article 2 granted not only a ten mile wide strip, but also other lands and waters outside the zone for the canal. Article 3 granted the U.S. all authority, rights and powers in the zone as "if it were sovereign of the territory." Finally, article 13 permitted the United States to import, duty free, all goods and materials "necessary and convenient" for U.S. employees, workmen, laborers and their families.

Significantly, the rights the United States obtained in securing Panama's independence differed little from the Platt Amendment imposed upon Cuba or its actions in the Dominican Republic. Each represented the larger objective of establishing hegemony in the Caribbean region to secure it from foreign intervention, because the local populations were judged incapable of doing so themselves. Also, the rights granted to the United States within the zone differed little from those offered previously by Colombia or by Nicaragua to private canal companies. Whereas the private projects failed, this one would not, and the application of those treaty rights would contribute to much animosity between the United States and Panama for the next seventy-four years.

THE YEARS OF YANKEE DOMINANCE: 1904-1933

With treaty in hand the United States government, from 1904 to 1914, overcame an enormous challenge. When the canal opened eleven days after the outbreak of World War I, some $380 million had been spent to complete this engineering marvel. But the North Americans did more than build a canal. They left an indelible imprint upon Panama.

Immediately, Washington policymakers were concerned with political turmoil. Panama's record of political instability matched that of other Caribbean and Central American republics that prompted the United States to devise a protective policy for the region before World War I. In 1904 Secretary of War William Howard Taft warned that the United States would not tolerate political violence in Panama, because it would interfere with the construction, operation and maintenance of the canal. Toward that end the U.S. directed the demilitarization of the republic's small army in 1904 and the establishment of a national police force in its place. In 1915 the U.S. Navy took away the rifles used by the police and, from then until the early 1930s, the United States provided a police instructor to supervise law enforcement in the republic. In addition to the broad treaty rights that permitted the United States to maintain public order in the republic, the North Americans pressured the Panamanians into legitimizing that privilege in article 136 of their constitution. In exercise of that police power, North Americans entered the republic in 1918, 1921 and 1925. The zone police commander also tried to control liquor sales and ban prostitution in the terminal cities.

From the start of the canal's construction, zone police assumed responsibility for security within the zone and the U.S. military for guarding the zone against external attack. By 1912, the zone police numbered 117 white Americans and 116 black West Indians, who kept peace within their respective racial groups. World War I prompted the United States to establish the Panama Canal Defense Department, an autonomous army unit, to provide for the canal's protection. On the basis of defending the canal, the U.S. also came to control radio and civil aviation in the republic. Canal security also meant that the United States interfered with Panamanian foreign policy, as in 1921 when it forced the republic to accept a boundary settlement in its dispute with Costa Rica. The North American interference in Panama's internal and external affairs left a bitter legacy.

Beyond security, the North Americans developed an attitude of protective paternalism toward Panamanian politics during the construction period. They wanted the Panamanian politicians to conduct themselves in a respectable and constitutional manner. The North Americans recognized that the Liberal and Conservative parties were little more than conglomerates of urban and rural families competing for political prominence. Apparently the North Americans favored the Conservatives over the Liberals because of the latter's appeal to the lower socio-economic groups in the terminal cities, but with time's passage any member of the local elite who was white, spoke English, was educated beyond high school, had traveled abroad and recognized U.S. dominance proved acceptable. The Panamanian elite recognized this too. A few of them secured "gold roll" appointments in the zone operations and others benefitted from canal related businesses. The cozy relationship with the North Americans did not prevent U.S. fear of political violence, which contributed to varying degrees of U.S. election supervision of the 1908 and 1912 presidential elections and congressional and municipal elections in 1906 and 1918. In effect, most Panamanian elite understood that the republic was not truly independent, but rather an extension of the Canal Zone.

North American interference in the republic was not all negative. During the canal construction period, the U.S. Army supervised public health programs that included water and sewage systems in the terminal cities, hospital construction and mosquito control. The first prevented the spread of bacterial diseases and the latter provided a healthier environment for the tens of thousands of canal laborers who lived outside the zone. The canal hospitals provided the first modern medical care in Panama and the mosquito control program protected all from insect diseases such as yellow fever and malaria. At the time, these accomplishments were overshadowed by U.S interference in Panamanian affairs and activities in the zone.

Panama lacked the human resources necessary for the canal's construction, when it began in 1904. Some 17,000 laborers were used, most of them imported from the Caribbean Islands. The number of immigrants was estimated at 200,000 when dependents and opportunists hoping to capitalize upon the canal project were included. The presence of such a large non-white labor group irritated the Panamanian elite, who tried to deport them. On the other hand, the U.S. authorities preferred the large labor pool, which translated into lower wages and less labor unrest. U.S. canal wage scales placed the Panamanians in the same category as the West Indians. The 5,300 North Americans were given a 25 percent wage differential to make the job attractive to them so far from home and they were paid in gold coin ("gold roll"), while 31,000 Panamanian and West Indian laborers received silver specie ("silver roll"). Those on the silver roll had little, if any, opportunity for job advancement. The wage policy added to the Panamanian discontent with the black West Indians.

Soon after construction began, two wage increases were granted in an effort to counter rising food and rent prices, but to no avail. Eggs reportedly sold for $1.50 per dozen and workers slipped into the jungle in search of food. In response, Canal Zone Governor Charles Magoon turned to the commissary operation. To provision the labor force some 2,000 miles from the U.S. mainland, refrigeration plants and freight cars were introduced.

The Panama Railroad company provided shipping discounts on the large quantities of supplies that came from the states, which also entered Panama exempt from import duties. Canal officials justified the sale of luxury items as necessary to keep the North American workers content. Without controls, the commissaries were open to anyone, whether a zone employee or not. Because neither Panama City nor Colón had sufficient housing for the bloated labor force, the canal authorities undertook housing projects to meet the workers's needs and for the North American technical staff, better homes were constructed to satisfy their expectations.

Throughout the construction period, the Panamanians correctly asserted that the commissaries sold luxury items (ie., silks and perfumes), that sales were not limited to zone workers and their families and that the commissary received special shipping rates from the states. When the canal opened to world traffic in 1914, sales were made to transiting ships. The U.S. authorities, over Panamanian protest, reasoned that ship sales were essential to the canal's operation. The government of Panama tried to control the situation in 1915 when it issued coupon books, so that beyond the laborers, only the republic's president, three other officials and eleven accredited foreign diplomats could use the commissary. In 1917, Secretary of State Robert Lansing asserted that the 1903 treaty did not empower Panama to charge tariffs on goods that passed through the republic to the zone.

During the construction period, U.S. private investors were permitted to engage in some of the construction projects, but as the canal neared completion, many moved into the republic where they competed with Panamanians. Among the most notable was Minor C. Keith who put together the United Fruit Company (UFCO) in 1899 and moved into the Bocas del Toro region northwest of Panama City, where the company relied upon the produce of private growers. When a leaf blight devastated the area after World War I, UFCO moved its operations to Chiriqui Province on the Pacific Coast, where production was on company lands, and the company accounted for the largest share of Panama's exports. Otherwise, the North Americans did little investing in the Panamanian economy. By 1920, they held about $10 million in direct investments and several million dollars in government bonds. To Panamanians, however, the United States had created a colony in their midst.

The ink had barely dried on the 1903 treaty, when the Panamanian protests began over the treaty's interpretation and implementation. For example, Foreign Minister Ricardo Alfaro declared that the United States intended to turn the zone into a center for world commerce at Panama's expense. He asserted that the application of U.S. tariffs on goods entering the zone and control of its ports of entry denied Panamanian agriculturalists and cattleman a ready market and that—if the United States imported foodstuffs from the states—they faced extinction. Alfaro also charged that treaty articles 3, 10 and 13 clearly limited U.S. sovereignty in the zone, including the control of commerce into the North American enclave.

President Theodore Roosevelt hoped to ease the tension by sending Secretary of War William Howard Taft to the republic in 1904, but declarations that the U.S. was motivated by a sense of justice toward Panama and that it did not intend to create a colony were coolly received. Taft eventually hammered out an executive agreement that provided for Panama's postal service to replace the U.S. system in the zone and that all goods not essential for the canal's construction to be subject to appropriate U.S. and Panamanian customs duties. The agreement authorized the Canal Zone governor to negotiate an agreement with the Panamanian government that would protect Panamanian commercial pursuits in the zone from unfair competition. Although the zone authorities agreed to purchase clothing and food in Panama, Taft warned that price gouging would lead to expansion of the commissary operation. That is exactly what happened and the Canal Zone developed into a self-sufficient economy.

Failing to gain access to the lucrative zone market, the Panamanian elite built rooming houses, saloons, brothels, restaurants and shops along the zone border to cater to soldiers and to the foreign labor force. But this proved insufficient to bolster the local economy. The Panamanians came to protest the amount of the annual annuity, pay differentials between North American and Panamanian workers, lack of employment opportunities for Panamanians, use of lands outside those specified in the 1903 treaty and, ultimately, the question of sovereignty. The sense of anti-American nationalism intensified as the 1920s approached. As did all Latin Americans, the Panamanians viewed the League of Nations as a vehicle to check U.S. imperialism, but became disenchanted with the organization when the North Americans refused to join.

Panamanian nationalism increased the demand for sovereignty over the zone. The Panamanians reasoned that the 1903 treaty was something hastily concluded under duress and that the leaders of the new republic did not comprehend the significance of the treaty in establishing a relationship which would prevent the republic from realizing the anticipated benefits of the canal. The Panamanians came to demand that the United States limit its activities to the operation, maintenance and defense of the canal and that the zone not be open to the world's commerce, so that Panama could capitalize upon its most precious resource, its location, and improve its prestige as a nation.

By the early 1920s, the North Americans were also disenchanted with the vagueness of the Hay-Bunau-Varilla Treaty. Canal Zone governors pointed out that changing circumstances, such as the development of radio, telegraphy and aircraft, required new explicitness. But U.S. officials refused to budge on their jurisdiction over the zone; they were determined only to define more clearly their rights.

When negotiations for a revision of the 1903 treaty commenced in March 1924, the Panamanian and North American delegates were at divergent poles. The talks dragged on to July 1926, interrupted by presidential elections and inaugurations. When the proposed treaties were completed, Panama gained only a sense of recognition of its rights over the zone. Delegates had come to Washington demanding severe restrictions on the commissary operation, but left with the consumption habits of some 8,500 zone workers and their families unchanged, ship sales untouched and no change in the shipping rates charged by the Panama Railroad for imported commissary goods. The Panamanian demand for a final determination of all lands outside the zone for canal use resulted in an agreement for joint consultation in determining the value of future confiscated lands. Other aspects of shared jurisdiction focused on radio, telegraphy, aircraft, custom houses, sanitation in the terminal cities and defense, but in each instance the North Americans remained the final arbiter. The North Americans achieved their objective of more clearly defined rights that reflected the changed circumstances since 1903. Nevertheless, the Panamanians appeared satisfied. One might ask why. The answer lay in the make up of Panamanian society. The traditional oligarchs, those first generation leaders who obtained independence, still curried favor with the North Americans. While they publicly responded to the nationalists' calls for Panamanian rights over the zone, the elite remained more interested in protecting their own position. They perceived any accommodation with Washington as a step in that direction.

President Rodolfo Chiari told the Panamanians that this was the best treaty that could be obtained under the circumstances and that it was at least preferable to the 1903 convention. Not everyone agreed. The local press asserted that the proposed treaty permitted the United States to exploit the republic's only resource without benefit to Panama. The people in Colón became apprehensive as they anticipated additional U.S. land confiscations there. By the time a committee of the National Assembly began its review of the treaty in December 1926, three groups of opposition had developed. One, centered around the Chamber of Commerce, decried the failure to gain access to the lucrative zone market. Two labor organizations, the *Federación Obrera* and the *Sindicato General de Trabajadores*, railed against the negotiators' failure to gain improvements in job opportunities for Panamanian (but not West Indian) workers. And a group of young writers affiliated with *Acción Communal* distributed fly sheets and other literature that played on anti-U.S. sentiment, particularly the agreement to place Panama on the U.S. side in any future war. The protests escalated into demonstrations and death threats against assemblymen who might approve the treaty, which prompted the National Assembly, on January 26, 1927, to suspend consideration of the proposed treaty until there existed an opportunity to negotiate changes that would satisfy Panama's national interests. The next day in Washington, the State Department publicly dismissed the treaty revision discussions as minor in character and not effecting the substance of the 1903 convention.

For both the North Americans and Panamanians the legacy of the failed treaty negotiations proved important. Each now understood that the demands of Panama's non-elite needed to be addressed. Merchants wanted measurable trade benefits, Panamanian laborers increased job opportunities and pay equalization, and land owners security against future expropriations. In addition to these canal operation issues, Washington's need to defend the waterway against advanced military weaponry required privileges that only further impinged upon Panamanian sovereignty.

DEALING WITH PANAMANIAN NATIONALISM: 1933-1968

Panama came away from the 1926 treaty negotiations more intent on pressing its demands, as witnessed in March 1927 and January 1928, when Foreign Minister Alfaro sought to reopen negotiations. Panama's recalcitrance contributed to the delay of signing a joint claims convention until March 1933. The global depression that began in late 1929 exacerbated Panama's already fragile economy, and the canal was seen locally as the source of all the nation's economic ills.

At the same time, there was movement for change in the United States. With the end of World War I, the European threat to the entire Caribbean lessened, contributing to the State Department's wish to withdraw from the policy of Caribbean interventions that dated to the turn of the century. Throughout the 1920s, the Democratic party continually criticized the incumbent Republicans for not acting to alter the imperialist perception. Criticism also came from abroad. The larger Latin American nations used the inter-American conferences at Santiago in 1923 and Havana in 1928 to lash out at the U.S. record in the Caribbean. The shift in U.S. policy became evident in 1928 with President-elect Herbert Hoover's goodwill visit to Central and South America. Subsequently, the J. Reuben Clark *Memorandum on the Monroe Doctrine* renounced U.S. intervention in Latin America's domestic affairs under the terms of the Roosevelt Corollary to the Monroe Doctrine. The policy change was complete with President Franklin D. Roosevelt's 1933 inaugural address in which he declared that hereafter the United States would act as a "Good Neighbor" and henceforth no longer intervene in its neighbors internal affairs. The policy shift impacted immediatly upon U.S.-Panamanian relations.

When Panamanian President Harmodio Arias came to Washington in October 1933, he found a receptive President Roosevelt awaiting him in the White House. Arias argued that Panama should be permitted a greater opportunity to exploit commercial advantages created by canal traffic and that unsettled economic conflicts should be submitted to an arbiter. Arias also asserted that the large West Indian presence threatened the republic's political and social tranquility and that the United States should help repatriate them. The joint communique issued at the end of their discussions reflected Panama's concerns.

Roosevelt directed that negotiations begin in early 1934 over objections from the War Department, which held that any further economic concessions would make the canal less secure, from Canal Zone authorities, who argued that the canal was not yet complete and that additional Panamanian lands would be needed for its protection and maintenance, and from Americans residing in the zone, who sought to protect their way of life. The Panamanian negotiators, Ricardo Alfaro and Narciso Garay, came to the table determined to achieve the demands made by Panamanian merchants and Panamanian laborers to end U.S.

land seizures and to raise the annual annuity to offset the decline in the value of the dollar. Although the State Department was prepared to make non-strategic concessions in order to promote better relations with all of Latin America, Secretary of State Cordell Hull and his staff focused on security, especially the future expropriation of land for defense purposes.

In 110 sessions, some of which were attended by Roosevelt, the details of a proposed new treaty were hammered out and finally signed on March 2, 1936. While the Panamanians did not achieve all of their objectives, they came away pleased with the abrogation of the U.S. protectorate over the republic as provided for in the 1903 treaty and an end to U.S. eminent domain over Panama City and Colón. The Panamanians gained recognition of joint sovereignty with the shared responsibility over future land acquisitions for canal purposes and control over radio stations. The restrictions placed upon commissary sales and the opportunity for Panamanian private businesses to enter the zone market gave the hope for increased prosperity to the Panamanian merchants. The adjustment of the annual annuity from $250,000 to $430,000 only reflected the devaluation of the U.S. dollar that Roosevelt had instituted as an anti-depression measure. But Panama had not asked for more. In an accompanying note, Roosevelt promised equal job opportunities for Panamanians in the zone, but nothing was mentioned about repatriation of the West Indians for which the president had indicated support in 1933. The treaty satisfied the desires of Panama's upper and middle sectors and Panamanian labor organizations. Therefore it won quick approval in the National Assembly. In 1936, unlike 1926 and 1927, the Panamanians did not assert that the pledge to cooperate in the canal's wartime defense could be broadly interpreted to impinge upon national sovereignty.

However, it was the defense issue that delayed U.S. ratification of the Hull-Alfaro Treaty until 1939. The War Department was reluctant to surrender control of radio communications and the ability to confiscate land for future canal operations, while the zone authorities resisted the equal opportunity labor provisions. The Senate finally caved into

White House pressure just prior to the 1939 inter-American conference on hemispheric defense to be held in Panama, but only after preserving the better paying Canal Zone jobs for North Americans.

From the time the Hull-Alfaro Treaty was signed in 1936 until its ratification in 1939, U.S. authorities became increasingly concerned with the rising war clouds in Europe and pondered hemispheric defense, including fifth column sabotage efforts. Canal officials concluded that the waterway was the jugular vein of hemispheric defense and was no longer immune to external attack because of the army fortifications—four 16-inch and six 6-inch guns on the Pacific entrance and a 16-inch and a 14-inch on the Caribbean and the presumably impenetrable jungle around the zone. Military technology had drastically altered since 1914. Aircraft carriers, and their aircraft, and submarines made these defense bastions obsolete. The presence of large German colonies in Central America and Colombia raised the specter of sabotage, a factor not present in World War I. To meet the changed conditions, the U.S. military began monitoring the German colonies in the region and the army began plans to intercept attackers in the Caribbean before they reached the canal. The War Department identified 71 sites in Panama needed for defense purposes, including interconnecting highways, over which it wanted complete control for 999 years!

Whatever spirit of cooperation existed in 1939 disappeared a year later when Ambassador William Dawson commenced negotiations for these defense sites. In October 1940, following the death of President Juan D. Arosemena, Arnulfo Arias ascended to the presidency. Representing the second generation of nationalist Panamanians, Arias asserted that there could be no transfer of authority for the defense sites until other issues were solved including the impact of the installations on Panama's security, the duration of jurisdiction over real estate owned by the Panama Railroad Company, smuggling between the bases and surrounding villages, zone commissaries, the completion of twelve public works projects, repatriation of the Jamaican laborers and their families and the promise that there would be no further immigration of people of the Negro race. Even if these issues were settled, Arias would extend the defense site leases only for the duration of a presidential term and Panama would retain criminal jurisdiction over persons on the sites with the exception of U.S. military personnel. Under these circumstances, no progress was made for nearly a year.

The situation changed after October 1941, when, during an unauthorized visit to Cuba, a bloodless coup d'etat ousted Arias and replaced him with Ricardo de la Guardia, who reportedly received encouragement from U.S. zone officials to change the presidency. Following Japan's attack at Pearl Harbor on December 7, 1941, Panama quickly declared war on the Axis powers and de la Guardia acknowledged his country's obligation under Article 9 of the 1936 convention for the defense of the canal. In May 1942, Panama concluded the defense sites agreement which granted the U.S. Army its needs and jurisdictional control over civilian and military personnel until one year after a definitive peace treaty ending the war was signed. The U.S. agreed to pay Panama a $50 per hectare rental for the defense sites except for the Rio Hato airbase, which was fixed at $10,000 per year. The U.S. also agreed to construct the inter-connecting highways, but stipulated that it would pay only one third of the subsequent maintenance costs.

By the terms of an accompanying executive agreement, the U.S. transferred control of water and sewage facilities of Panama City to the republic, relinquished real estate owned by the Panama Railroad Company, paid Panama's share of the Rio Hato highway and promised the construction of a cross-canal bridge after the war. Although these agreements were honored, Panama was never satisfied because the United States remained obsessed with the defense of the canal rather than the republic's economic development. The United States, however, did not bend to the Panamanian demand to repatriate West Indians and to refrain from using other minority ethnic laborers in the zone, a practice that the Panamanians found objectionable.

Before Pearl Harbor, reports circulated about a Nazi clique which threatened to spread pro-Axis propaganda and possibly sabotage the canal. Since the early twentieth century, people from Germany and Italy had entered the country easily and obtained provisional naturalization, providing them with legal protection, although they were never required to complete the naturalization process. In the 1930s, the German and Italian consulates became propaganda centers and allegedly the operations centers for sabotage plans. A number of influential Panamanians, including Arnulfo Arias, were linked to the Axis cause. Arias' link made him unpopular with U.S. officials and contributed to zone officials' connection to his overthrow in October 1941. After Pearl Harbor, the Panamanian government cooperated with the detention of some 1,200 citizens of Axis nations. After screening, most were released, but 327 persons suspected of espionage were deported to the United States where they were interned for the war's duration. Those who stayed in Panama were subject to strict surveillance, censorship of their mail and other restrictive measures. For the United States, the fifth column threat had been eliminated.

Throughout the war, President de la Guardia took every opportunity to exhort his people to the allied cause. The government did not protest the U.S. naval patrol of the coastal areas, particularly during the height of the German U-boat campaign in the Caribbean during 1942, nor the ban on fishing within twenty-five miles of Panama's shoreline. U.S. military personnel were treated cordially as they passed through enroute to the Pacific. Newspapers deplored the early Axis victories, praised the Allied cause and later applauded the Allied, particularly the U.S., military successes.

The war had a mixed impact upon the Panamanian economy. Over 6,500 acres of hemp producing abaca were developed in the Bocas del Toro region and mahogany woods were exported for war purposes. The United States bought the complete output of Panamanian crude rubber. U.S. merchant ships registered under Panama's flag to circumvent pre-war neutrality legislation continued that status after the war, effectively increasing the Panamanian merchant fleet to over two million tons. The construction of the defense sites, highways and work on a third set of locks demanded an increased labor force that Panama could not meet. To meet this need, zone officials recruited Puerto Ricans, Colombians, Costa Ricans, El Salvadorans and Cubans and reached an agreement with Great Britain that provided for the introduction of several thousand Jamaican laborers, who were to be housed in the zone and repatriated at the war's end. Many Panamanian sensibilities were inflamed by these actions, but the elite benefitted because the construction boom increased their number on the zone's "gold roll" and with the expanded number of wartime "silver roll" employees, demands for housing, food and services increased in the republic. With the increase in zone labor and in the military transiting the canal, Panama's agricultural sector strained, but could not satisfy the demand for foodstuffs, thus prompting the State Department to reach agreements with other Central American countries, particularly Costa Rica. Taken together, these economic developments had a positive impact upon Panama and gave hope that the post war period would be one of continued prosperity.

But there were ominous signs that all was not well. Toward the war's end, some Panamanian leaders warned that the republic would not return to its subservient status. Panamanian merchants still viewed the commissary operation as a source of unfair competition. Most galling was the stark contrast between the lush living styles of the American workers in the zone and the Panamanians, particularly in the adjacent areas at Panama City and Colón. Also, West Indian laborers began to place responsibility on the United States for the racial discrimination they suffered at the hands of the Panamanians and admonished Washington for not working to improve their civil status in the republic.

The Panama at the end of World War II was quite different from the one at the end of World War I. So, too, was the U.S. presence. The Panamanians had become better educated, making them more qualified for better paying jobs in the Canal Zone and the private sector. A new generation of West Indian labor leaders emerged determined to win better wages and benefits from the Canal Zone employers. They soon found a sympathetic ear in

Panama's political arena. These pressures came at a time when Panama was entering an economic downturn as the demands generated by World War II declined. For all Panamanians there was the lingering sovereignty issue, best demonstrated by the defense sites.

Amid Panama's growing anti-American sentiment, the U.S. military establishment viewed Panama as an outlying military post with growing importance to hemispheric defense. The Commerce Department continued to view the republic as a transit route vital to the national economy and world commerce and the State Department saw the republic as a remnant of an imperial age.

The U.S. military had constructed 134 defense sites in Panama during the war and wanted to retain several of them in the postwar period. The military also advocated the construction of a new canal because many of its newer capital ships could not transit the existing waterway and, even with wider locks, the resultant bottleneck would expose the ships to air assault. Surging Panamanian nationalism conflicted with U.S. security interests, a fact that President Enrique Jiménez failed to grasp when he initialled an agreement extending the U.S. occupation of the defense sites for ten years. A wide range of people from the middle sector—students, technocrats, laborers, managers, shopkeepers—used the defense sites issue to demand a greater share of the Canal Zone "gold roll" jobs, the commissary market and recognition of Panamanian sovereignty over the zone. In scenes reminiscent of the violent response to the proposed 1926 treaties, they marched on the National Assembly and, as twenty years before, in December 1947 the Assembly unanimously rejected the proposed extension.

The Panamanian economy also suffered from the post-war U.S. demobilization and declining canal traffic. By the time the defense sites shut down in 1948 (except the sprawling Rio Hato air base), the economy was in full recession. The situation worsened in the 1950s when the U.S. government introduced austerity measures into the Canal Zone operations. Low cost housing and social services for non-U.S. citizen employees were cut, forcing thousands of families to face a higher cost of living in the terminal cities. Decisions in Washington contributed to a sense of Panamanian national unity that placed responsibility upon the zone for all of the country's ills. In addition to the discontent over the impact of the zone, the masses now openly questioned the traditional relationship between the Panamanian elite and U.S. authorities.

By the time Dwight D. Eisenhower was elected president in 1952, United States policymakers had determined that there was a Soviet inspired global communist menace. Given this attitude, Washington feared communists might capitalize upon Panama's economic plight and nationalistic desire to control the canal. In response, the Eisenhower administration provided an average of $7 million annually in economic development assistance (largely for infrastructure projects) to the Remón administration and welcomed his National Guard officers into the School of the Americas in the Canal Zone where the U.S. military trained Latin American officers.

Remón also realized he could use this threat and Panama's strident nationalism to forge a new treaty with the United States. In 1953 he pleaded Panama's case directly to President Eisenhower. His demands included implementation of the equal employment opportunities promised in 1936, power to tax Panamanian Canal Zone employees, elimination of commissary contraband sales, increased purchases of Panamanian goods by zone authorities, a share of Canal Zone profits, the equal display of each country's flags and explicit recognition of Panama's sovereignty over the zone. To press these issues, Remón orchestrated demonstrations in Panama City, a precedent setting tactic to exert pressure upon the United States. Eisenhower appeared receptive, at least to the republic's economic rights in the Canal Zone.

Subsequent negotiations led to a new treaty that was signed in January 1955. For Panama it was a marked improvement over the 1903 and 1936 accords. The annual annuity was increased to $1.9 million, commissary sales were further restricted, the railroad properties in Panama City and Colón returned to the republic, the long awaited trans-canal bridge was to be built at U.S. expense and there was a promise to equalize salaries. In addition, the Panamanian government gained the right to tax its citizens employed in the zone and to administer sanitation in the terminal cities. For the United States, the treaty provided for the continued lease of the Rio Hato air base.

Understandably, the Panamanian legislature quickly ratified the agreement. The United States Senate gave its approval, but not before hearing protests from several special interest groups. Shippers expressed fear that the higher annuity would prompt increased canal charges. Zonians protested salary equity and the potential loss of jobs to Panamanians. The military wanted continued assurance that its defense rights would not be sacrificed. Finally, a coterie of nationalists did not want anything changed from the 1903 treaty.

Remón did not live to see the new treaty implemented. He was machine gunned to death on January 2, 1955. Had he lived, he certainly would have been disappointed because, in application, Panama failed to receive all the treaty had promised. Panama's treasury gained from the increased annuity and taxes and local merchants from increased sales, but canal authorities continued to purchase most of their supplies elsewhere.. The U.S. Congress belatedly made a halfhearted effort at equal employment opportunities. Subsequently, Secretary of State John Foster Dulles thwarted every Panamanian effort to assert sovereignty over the zone. Within the republic, the West Indian descendants who had become Panamanian citizens, paid a high price. They lost commissary and housing privileges and began paying income taxes.

At the time of the 1955 treaty, the strategic value of the Canal Zone had appreciably altered because of its vulnerability to attack by modern weapons and its inability to accommodate larger naval vessels. Still, the U.S. military had expanded its facilities within the Canal Zone, making Rio Hato Air Base the only desired defense site outside the zone. Rather than defense of the canal, the zone had become a strategic post for U.S. hemispheric security. Its value lay in its jungle warfare school, intelligence operations, informal inter-American defense network and the facilities to deploy troops quickly to anywhere in the hemisphere. The Pentagon needed the Canal Zone, not for itself, but for the bases it had there. The Panamanians were not pleased that the new defense requirements had contributed to an increased U.S. military presence in the zone.

The conflict of U.S. and Panamanian interests intensified under Remón's successor, Ernesto de la Guardia. He and his Foreign Secretary, Aquilino Boyd, and Ambassador to Washington, Ricardo Arías, were sharp critics of U.S. canal policy. Influenced by the shortcomings of the 1955 treaties, by Egypt's seizure of the Suez Canal and Venezuela's new arrangements with foreign owned oil companies, they demanded a fifty-fifty split in canal toll revenues, $40 million in short term economic development assistance, rapid implementation of the 1955 wage agreement and better paying jobs for Panamanians in the zone. While the government pursued diplomacy, the Panamanian people took to the streets. In May 1958, when students planted Panamanian flags in the zone during demonstrations calling for Panamanian sovereignty, the National Guard killed one student in suppressing the riots. Fidel Castro's December victory in Cuba set off another round of demonstrations. In October 1959, laborers demonstrated in Panama City, demanding higher wages, price controls, rent ceilings, low cost housing, unemployment insurance and land reform. The unrest spread to the Canal Zone on Panama's independence day, November 3, when a group of students and politicians again entered the zone to raise their flag and assert Panama's sovereignty over it. In the ensuing violence, American buildings were destroyed by fire and several demonstrators injured. A month later, another set of riots broke out, only to be suppressed by the Panamanian National Guard. For some Panamanians, demonstrations were not enough. On three occasions in 1959, Panamanian insurgents, accompanied by Cuban militiamen, invaded the country in hopes of toppling the elected government.

Initially, Eisenhower's sympathy toward Panama rested with the historic injustices legitimized by an unequal treaty system, but following Castro's revolution in Cuba, Nixon's ill-fated trip to Latin America and the prodding of Brazilian President Juscelino Kubitschek, Eisenhower recognized the need to address the social and economic disparities that plagued Panama. The establishment of the Inter-American Development Bank and the Social Security Progress Trust Fund signaled the forthcoming of the Alliance for Progress. For Panama, it meant an immediate $6 million increase in assistance for low cost housing, new water supply systems in Panama City and in the Canal Zone, increased wages for Panamanian unskilled and semi-skilled workers in the zone, training of Panamanians for higher level positions and jobs reclassification from the local rate to the U.S. rate. Eisenhower also directed the flying of the Panamanian flag in the zone as an effort to mollify Panamanian sensitivity.

Roberto Chiari in Panama and John F. Kennedy in the United States came to their presidencies holding similar beliefs that economic and social disparities were breeding grounds for communists. Chiari needed to convince his elitist colleagues of this view, while Kennedy's vision in the Alliance for Progress had to be tempered in Panama by U.S. security interests on the isthmus and the popular perception that the Canal Zone was an integral part of the United States. The two discussed these issues when they met in Washington in June 1962.

On the canal issue, however, Kennedy moved too slowly for Chiari. In 1961 an interdepartmental committee recommended increased tangible benefits to Panama, but decided that any treaty revision would have to await the outcome of a study for a new sea level canal. Kennedy also approved a memorandum calling for the drafting of a new treaty, but did not inform Chiari that he had approved it. Instead, Kennedy took public actions in an effort to assuage Panamanian nationalism. In 1962 he used the opening of the cross-canal bridge to announce that the Panamanian flag should fly at fifteen canal sites, and later that same year he authorized a joint four-man commission to discuss the broad range of issues dividing the two countries.

None of Kennedy's public actions aided Chiari in defusing Panamanian frustrations. In fact, the tension increased when a U.S. zonian sued to prevent the joint flag flying, Congress failed to appropriate funds for the study of a new sea level canal and, the State Department failed to replace the popular Ambassador Joseph MacFarland after his resignation in August 1963. These actions only confirmed the Panamanian suspicions that the United States had no intention of addressing the republic's needs. Relations drifted until January 9, 1964, when a group of Panamanian students marched to Balboa High School in the zone to raise their flag. Although the school was designated by Kennedy as one of the fifteen sites, the defiant zonians had resisted. The confrontation turned into four days of violence in which over two dozen persons were killed, scores more injured and thousands of dollars of U.S. property in Panama destroyed by fire. In face of the violence, Chiari severed diplomatic relations with the United States. President Lyndon B. Johnson responded by halting U.S. economic assistance to the republic.

Panama charged that the U.S. forces used brutality during the riots and demanded that the Organization of American States (OAS) investigate the crisis, which only confirmed Johnson's suspicion that Chiari was attempting to use the riots to force concessions from the United States. Given this atmosphere, Johnson refused to discuss any canal issue until full diplomatic relations were restored. A stalemate persisted for the next two months during which the OAS failed to effect a mediation of the conflict and, Panama's economy continued to deteriorate due to the loss of U.S. government aid and a halt in private investment. Chiari's hand was further weakened when he learned of a Defense Department report that urged Johnson to pursue the construction of a sea level canal somewhere else in Central America. Forced into a corner by these events, Chiari caved in and, on April 3, agreed to the resumption of diplomatic relations.

Despite his strong stand, President Johnson understood that the 1964 riots demonstrated the need to reassess the U.S. position. He understood the canal's vulnerability to attack and sabotage, the underdevelopment of Panama's economy and the concomitant social ills that fueled Panama's determination to end the sovereignty clauses found in the 1903 treaty. When bilateral talks began in July 1964, each nation stated its traditional position: Panama demanding sovereignty over the zone and the United States unwilling to surrender control. As could be expected, the talks quickly stalemated. In December 1964 Johnson attempted to break the stalemate with a proposal that the United States would negotiate a new treaty with Panama while simultaneously proceeding with plans to build a new canal. Although a newly appointed commission was given four years to examine possible locations, Johnson suggested the old San Juan River route, Colombia and Panama as potential sites for the new canal. New Panamanian President Marcos Robles was not moved by Johnson's flaunting of power. He understood that Johnson's threat of a new canal was intended to force Panama's hand. Robles refused to consider the offer.

While Johnson cajoled and Robles stood firm,, the negotiators, reached an agreement by September 1965 on a range of issues to be discussed, including the abrogation of the 1903 treaty. Talks continued to drag on for two years until June 1967, when three draft treaties were completed. The first draft treaty met Panama's major demands. It provided for abrogation of the 1903 treaty and provided for the cooperative administration of the canal by a joint commission composed of five North Americans and four Panamanians appointed by the U.S. president. Most of the lands in the zone would be returned to Panama and the smaller zone that replaced the original one would have a government limited to basic services. Panama would derive new revenues from the canal. The treaty would expire on December 31, 1999 or, one year after the completion of a sea level canal, whichever came first. The second draft treaty provided for joint Panamanian-U.S. defense of the canal into the twenty first century. The final treaty permitted the United States alone, or in a consortium, to construct a sea-level canal to be administered in the same bi-national fashion proposed in the first draft treaty for the existing structure. While these draft treaties would have granted Panama its sovereignty over the canal, the United States did not come away empty handed. The joint commission secured Washington's administrative position and the defense treaty guaranteed its security interests for up to 100 years.

When the draft treaties were leaked by the local press, the Panamanian people were not pleased. Robles was accused of selling out to the North Americans. The press correctly pointed out that the proposed treaties granted Panama *de jure* recognition of its sovereignty over the zone, but that the United States retained *de facto* control. Shortly thereafter, the canal issue became entwined in the domestic politics of both Panama and the United States. In Panama, the frustration with elitist politics resulted in the election of Arnulfo Arias, but his effort to control the military led to his subsequent overthrow in October 1968 by Omar Torrijos, a man who understood Panama's emotional state regarding the canal. In the United States, Lyndon Johnson, pained by the agony of Vietnam and the domestic disruptions, refused to seek the presidency for a second term. The 1968 election brought Richard Nixon to the White House, and he arrived without a clearly defined Latin American policy. In effect, Nixon placed the canal issue on the proverbial back burner.

TORRIJOS, NIXON AND CARTER: 1968-1980

During his first administration, Richard Nixon generally ignored the Panama problem. Unlike Johnson, the Nixon team did not believe that the canal arrangement needed to be altered. The administration steadfastly clung to two traditional non-negotiable issues: (1) that the U.S. maintain control of the canal operation and (2) that the U.S. preserve the right unilaterally to defend the canal. Like many of his predecessors, Nixon remained convinced that if some economic concessions were made to Panama, the crisis would pass.

But the crisis did not pass. After consolidating his power, in early 1969, Torrijos signaled Washington that he was willing to resume negotiations based upon the three 1967 draft treaties.

When he learned that Nixon would not deal with his "military type, provisional government," Torrijos withdrew the offer. With time's passage, both Torrijos and Nixon confronted new pressures that brought the canal issue back to the forefront. In Panama, wealthy landowners opposed land expropriation programs, the business community was frustrated by a stagnant economy and everyone opposed the National Guard's arrogance and unchecked violation of human and civil rights. Many observers believed that these factors forced Torrijos to seek the conclusion of a new canal treaty in order to save his regime.

The Nixon administration faced a series of problems that weakened the U.S. position. The continuing conflict in Vietnam, the attack on the U.S. dollar in the international financial markets and the weakening U.S. economy tarnished the administration's image. Vis-a-vis Panama, Nixon was dealt a severe blow in November 1970 when the Atlantic-Pacific Interoceanic Canal Study Commission, established six years earlier by Lyndon Johnson, reported that Panama was the most suitable location for a new sea level canal that could be constructed for an estimated $3-4 billion. Apparently unaware of the changed environment, Nixon dismissed the report and said that he was interested only in a simple revision of the 1903 treaty.

Torrijos better understood the new conditions and used them to his advantage. He internationalized the canal issue by first consulting with traditional U.S. allies in the Caribbean region—Venezuela, Colombia and Costa Rica—and next by appealing to Peru and Cuba. Torrijos trekked off to Havana to meet personally with Castro. With both friend and foe of the United States, Torrijos forged a coalition that supported Panama's call for ownership of the canal. At the United Nations, where Panama occupied one of the elective seats on the Security Council, Foreign Minister Juan Antonio Tack and Ambassador Aquilino Boyd convinced several delegates of the correctness of the Panamanian cause. By November 1972, the weight of international opinion favored Panama and supported its request to hold a Security Council meeting in Panama City. The U.S. stood alone in opposition.

When the Security Council convened in Panama in March 1973, Torrijos immediately issued warnings that Panamanian frustration with U.S. intransigence over the colony it had created in the republic's midst would soon erupt into violence. Before the meeting ended, Peru co-sponsored with Panama a resolution that called for the quick conclusion of a new treaty that would fulfill Panama's legitimate aspirations and guarantee full respect for Panama's effective sovereignty over all of its territory. The U.S. was stung. It alone voted no, while its traditional ally, Great Britain, abstained. The other thirteen members voted for the resolution. Even Henry Kissinger acknowledged that the Panamanians had scored a major victory.

The Security Council meeting in Panama prompted the Nixon administration to alter its Panama policy. No longer would a simple solution suffice. The administration recognized that a continuation of the status quo threatened the canal's efficient operation and security. Within two months of the Panama meeting, the National Security Council (NSC) prepared a report for Nixon to present to Congress. The NSC recognized that the time had come to establish a new relationship with Panama.

In addition to the United Nations Security Council resolution and the NSC report, Panama was encouraged by events in the developing world. The Vietnamese conflict supported the assertion that the weak could defeat the strong if they remained persistent. The 1973 Arab-Israeli War further demonstrated the strength of Third World opinion against the United States and if the Organization of Petroleum Exporting Countries (OPEC) could reap the benefits of their natural resource-oil, by extension, so too, could Panama reap the benefits of its major resource-the canal.

The Panamanians again seized the initiative. Foreign Minister Tack sent a nine page letter to Secretary of State William P. Rogers, in which he argued that the 1903 treaty be replaced by one with a fixed termination date and formal recognition of Panama's sovereignty and jurisdiction over the zone and its infrastructure. In return for an equitable share of the profits, Panama would grant the United States the power to manage and protect the canal. The two countries would agree upon terms for the construction of a sea level canal. Finally, in 1974, after Kissinger became Secretary of State and veteran diplomat Ellsworth Bunker became chief U.S. negotiator, the United States accepted the Tack principles as the starting point for negotiations with Panama.

In the United States, acceptance of the Tack principles did not mean the rapid conclusion and ratification of a new treaty because of a forceful group of vocal opponents. Senator Strom Thurmond (R, S.C.) led a group of 38 senators who approved a resolution opposing Panamanian sovereignty over the canal. Facing possible impeachment proceedings stemming from the Watergate crisis, Nixon could not afford to antagonize them. The canal issue highlighted the Republican party's 1976 presidential primary campaign when Ronald Reagan, positioning himself to challenge Ford for the party's nomination, came out against any treaty that limited U.S. rights and privileges in the Canal Zone. He found a receptive audience. Given the extent of the opposition and in an effort to strengthen Ford's nomination bid, Secretary of State Kissinger declared that the United States needed to maintain its right to defend the canal for an indefinite period.

Frustrated with U.S. actions and confronted with increased opposition at home as the Panamanian economy continued to deteriorate, Torrijos resorted to the old tactics of threatening violence and coalition building. In early 1976 he orchestrated demonstrations in front of the U.S. embassy in Panama City, while the National Guard looked on approvingly. He also visited Cuba. But instead of forcing a U.S. retreat as in the past, these tactics stiffened U.S. resistance to further negotiations. Even the Democratic party's presidential candidate, Jimmy Carter, declared in June 1976, that he would not give up the Panama Canal as long as it remained important to national security. Again, it appeared that the two sides were back at square one.

The cloud of pessimism that hovered over the canal issue disappeared shortly after Carter's election victory in November 1976. He indicated that the Panama problem should be resolved quickly, a position reiterated by Secretary of State designee Cyrus Vance. Both had come to grasp the intensity of Panamanian frustration and realized that the threat of violence and potential sabotage endangered the canal. Carter also understood that continued failure to resolve the canal issue damaged the U.S. position in Latin America. Treaty prospects brightened in January 1977, when Carter tapped Sol Linowitz to be co-negotiator with Bunker. Linowitz, who headed the privately funded Commission on United States-Latin American Relations, argued that a more just treaty would serve as a catalyst to improved U.S.-Latin American relations. The Linowitz position was supported by the heads of state of Colombia, Costa Rica, Guatemala, Honduras, Mexico, Nicaragua and Venezuela who sent a joint communique to Carter shortly after his inauguration. The State Department joined the chorus calling for a new treaty. It argued that, despite all his weaknesses, Torrijos offered the best hope for a just settlement. The Department feared that should Torrijos be ousted, a more recalcitrant leader might emerge, making negotiations impossible and violence more probable.

What proved to be the final round of talks began in February 1977. The two most fundamental issues were a termination date for the U.S. control of the canal and the matter of access to and defense of the canal after the U.S. withdrawal. Secondary issues included the status of the U.S. forces in the Canal Zone, the question of jurisdiction of lands and waters, and technical questions pertaining to joint administration and operation of the canal. Finally, the two countries reached agreement on August 11th. Carter and Torrijos signed the treaties on September 7, 1977, in a Washington ceremony attended by most Latin American heads of state.

While the treaties satisfied Panama's long standing nationalistic demand for control of the canal, critics in Panama found several shortcomings in the treaties. For example, while Panamanian jurisdiction over the zone would occur three years after the treaties ratification, the United States retained the right to all land necessary for the canal's operations and defense until the year 2000. During the intervening years, a new nine member commission would be created to administer the canal operations, but only four Panamanians would serve and, then, only on Washington's approval. While the Panamanians could take over the commissary operations, zonians retained the U.S. government jobs that related to the canal operation. The North Americans retained the right to defend the canal until the year 2000 and, after that, the permanent right to defend the canal's neutrality. The toll structure was reconfigured so that the Panamanian government would receive thirty cents per ton on ships and cargo and up to another $20 million in canal toll revenues annually, if available. In addition to the treaties economic provisions, Carter agreed to a $295 million five year package of economic loans and guarantees and another $50 million in military assistance for ten years, but he rejected Torrijos' demand for an immediate $1 billion grant to stimulate the Panamanian economy.

Carter had made it clear that the U.S. Senate would not consent to the treaties without Panama's prior acceptance. Torrijos acted quickly. He conducted a national plebiscite on October 23, 1977, in which two-thirds of the Panamanians registered their approval. The approval reflected Panama's socio-economic structure. The elite saw the treaties as satisfying their longstanding demand for sovereignty over the Canal Zone and, with it, the opportunity for important management positions. They and the local merchants also realized that the door was now opened to the zone markets and other economic opportunities. For the Panamanian labor force, its hope for improved jobs and wages appeared satisfied. The losers, as they always had been, were the West Indians and their descendants. The Panamanian government had never done anything for them, and the new treaties failed to protect them from future Panamanian discrimination in the operation of the canal.

If Panamanian nationalism demanded control of the canal, United States nationalism demanded retention of the waterway. Public opinion polls in mid-August 1977 showed that 78 percent of the North Americans did not want to give up the canal. Both the proponents and opponents mobilized their resources for a great debate that engulfed the nation until late September 1979 when Congress gave its approval. The intervening debate focused on four key issues: (1) sovereignty over the zone, (2) the character of the Panamanian government, (3) U.S. defense needs and (4) economic importance of the canal.

Both proponents and opponents traced the origins of the sovereignty issue to the 1903 Hay-Bunau Varilla Treaty. Treaty supporters argued that the treaty granted the United States jurisdiction, not sovereignty, over the zone in return for an annual annuity. President Theodore Roosevelt, Secretary of War William Howard Taft and Secretary of State John Hay had acknowledged this. The latter coined the phrase "titular sovereignty," under which the United States constructed, operated and maintained the canal. In the treaty system that followed, the United States sought to clarify its rights for the more efficient operation, maintenance and defense of the canal. In contrast, treaty opponents asserted that Panama received $10 million for the 550 square mile territory and that the United States subsequently paid an additional $160 million for all privately owned land in the zone. By its own law, in 1904, Panama acknowledged the cession of the zone to the United States. Thereafter, the opponents asserted, the relinquishment of rights—sharing authority, restricting the commissaries, flying flags—only misled public opinion in both countries to believe that Panama had residual sovereignty.

Treaty supporters saw themselves as enlightened leaders, responding to the contemporary changing world relationships which recognized the aspirations of the less developed nations. They argued that the oligarchs who had traditionally ruled Panama demonstrated interests in the lower socio-economic groups only at election time or in treaty negotiations with the United States. The disparity of wealth and concomitant social inequalities, along with a corrupt political system, contributed to the ever increasing political instability that characterized Panamanian history. While the oligarchs had previously suppressed spokesman of the disenfranchised, like Arnulfo

Arias, they could not control Omar Torrijos. In contrast, treaty opponents saw little difference between the preceding oligarchs and Torrijos. They all were repressive and threatened to use the masses against the United States interests in the zone. Torrijos was even more dangerous, they argued, because of his links to Panamanian radicals and visits to Fidel Castro in Cuba. The oligarchs were preferable to the military despot.

The defense argument focused on potential future military needs and the ever present threat of sabotage. Historically, the canal provided an indispensable link in the security of the western hemisphere and the Caribbean-Gulf of Mexico sea-lanes. Although it acknowledged that the navy could better function with U.S. control of the canal, the Pentagon reluctantly supported the 1977 treaties, provided the United States was guaranteed access to the passageway, in order to meet the needs of a general war situation. In a conventional war, the Atlantic sea-lanes could be protected from bases at Puerto Rico and Guantánamo and the Pacific from the continental United States. In case of a nuclear attack, canal defense would be virtually impossible. After 2000, the Pentagon hoped that the right of "expeditious passage" would satisfy the need to move ships rapidly. The treaty supporters were encouraged by Torrijos' acknowledgement that the canal would be "under the protective umbrella of the Pentagon." U.S. military officials also reasoned that acceptance of the treaties would make the Panamanian government more friendly, thus reducing the possibility of attacks from jungle terrain. Treaty opponents focused on the need for the canal to serve a two ocean navy. They pointed out that nearly ninety percent of the U.S. fleet could still transit the canal and that only the newer aircraft carriers could not. They also argued that the canal, as an important world communications link, would not be subjected to a nuclear attack before an adversary struck at stateside industrial and military sites. Opponents also objected to the loss of the jungle warfare training facilities considered vital to Latin American defense strategies and feared the increased possibility of canal sabotage with the decline in the presence of U.S. troops.

Economically, the canal had importance to both Panama and world commerce. The Panamanians long maintained that their economy had not developed to its full potential because of the way the United States controlled the canal. Until post World War II, Panama's economy differed little from 1903. After the war, efforts were made to modernize the agricultural sector and to develop an industrial-commercial base. Still, in 1968 Torrijos inherited an underdeveloped economy with all its limitations. Treaty proponents argued that the economic provisions of the agreement offered much to improve the Panamanian economy so that the disparity of wealth and concomitant social inequalities would be alleviated. Because the bulk of the monies to accomplish this transition were to come from canal revenues and international institutions, not U.S. tax dollars, they asserted that Panama could serve as a model for the rest of Latin America. Critics, however, charged that the proposed investment was excessive and wasteful, given the plight of Panama's economy in 1976: a $2 billion national debt, which took up 39 percent of government revenues; a twelve percent nationwide unemployment rate and government mismanagement of national industries.

Both supporters and opponents placed emphasis upon the importance of the canal to U.S. trade and to world maritime traffic. Although U.S. intra-coastal trade was the most dominant route prior to World War II, new trends surfaced by the 1970s. The most significant route now was between Japan and the east coast of the United States and the second most traveled route connected the U.S. east coast with the west coast of Latin America. United States intra-coastal trade dropped to fifth place. These trends demonstrated the increasing economic interdependence of the world and led treaty supporters to argue that Panama could expect to recover operating costs and make a fair profit to use for domestic projects. Panama would not seek excessive profits, the proponents asserted, because it would be self defeating since it would result in the readjustment of trade routes, as demonstrated by the 1967 closure of the Suez Canal. For the same reasons Panama would need to operate the canal efficiently and smoothly. Treaty critics were not so optimistic. They feared that Panama would not be capable of maintaining efficient canal operations due to a lack of trained personnel, deterioration of maintenance and failure to make capital improvements. They feared the imposition of excessive tolls which would prove disastrous when passed on to consumers. Most of all, treaty opponents feared a closure. They pointed out that a closure of the canal would result in a 71 percent increase in fuel use by U.S. carriers, which translated into an estimated $932 million increase in the price of goods imported from abroad. For them, the question focused on who could control the canal more equitably and more efficiently for the benefit of world commerce.

When the U.S. Congress finally approved the treaties in late 1979, it removed a vestige of Colónialism, recognized the historic facts regarding sovereignty, the interdependence of world commerce and the changing nature of military defense, but it could not anticipate the future of Panamanian politics.

DEALING WITH A DICTATOR: MANUEL NORIEGA, 1980-1989

The implementation of the Panama Canal Treaties was left to others. In Panama, Torrijos' death in 1981 led to the emergence of Manuel Noriega. In the United States, Ronald Reagan replaced Jimmy Carter in the White House. Noriega and Reagan had their own agendas and soon found themselves at odds with each other.

Despite the developing conflict, implementation of the treaties went smoothly, at least in the beginning, thanks to the work of the U.S. Panama Canal administrator Lieutenant General Denis McAuliffe and Panamanian deputy administrator Fernando Manfredo. They inaugurated the tranisthmian oil pipeline, which helped to offset the lost canal revenues caused by the 1983 recession. They implemented a training program for Panamanians to take over the canal's skilled labor positions, introduced more equitable pay scales and turned over to the republic police and juridical responsibilities. Many of the resident North Americans, who lost jobs and special privileges, opted to return to the United States.

The harmonious relations at the top did not extend to the Panama Review Committee or Canal Board of Directors, where mutual jealousies and turf battles marred the work. The U.S. Congress, particularly after 1986, was slow to transfer canal operational profits to the republic and to appropriate funds for canal projects such as dredging and lock overhaul. Finally, as Panama's political turmoil intensified throughout the decade, U.S. officials became reluctant to prepare Panama to handle containerized ships, considered the maritime cargo carriers of the future.

During the first Reagan administration, it averaged $11 million in development assistance and $4 million in military aid and, in 1985 soared to $112 and $27 million respectively. The increased economic assistance was a clear indication that the Reagan administration wanted President Nicólas Ardito Barletta to succeed. Military assistance did not reflect a policy to professionalize the Panamanian Defense Forces (PDF), however, but rather the fact that Panama had to become a conduit for aid to the Nicaraguan contras at a time when Congress officially banned such assistance. After 1986, as United States-Panamanian relations steadily declined to a new low point, economic and military aid was reduced to a trickle and Panama was left off the list of nations eligible for assistance under the Caribbean Basin Initiative.

The reason for the deterioration in relations was Manuel Noriega, who became commander-in-chief of the National Guard in 1983 and quickly became Panama's dominant political figure. Noriega had been a CIA informant for fourteen years, and at the same time cooperating with regional drug traffickers. Reportedly, because of his value as an informant, President Richard Nixon had rebuffed a suggestion in 1972 that the CIA assassinate him. Noriega came to serve the infamous Medillín drug cartel by permitting it, for a price, to use Panama as a transhipment point and to recycle their monies through the republic's state bank. He also sold visas and passports to Chinese, Libyans and Cubans so that they could make their way to the United States. He participated in the transfer of U.S. high tech equipment to Cuba and the Soviet Union. Not one to spurn a profit, Noriega capitalized on the U.S. congressional ban on aid to the Nicaraguan contras by airlifting supplies to them. He also bought arms from Cuba and sold them to leftist guerrillas in El Salvador. Despite the evidence of activities inimical to U.S. interests, the Reagan administration did not interfere with Noriega because of his role in supporting the contras.

That changed after 1985, when Panamanian President Barletta decided to investigate the brutal slaying of human rights activist Hugo Spadafora and the *New York Times* published a series of articles by Seymour Hersch that detailed Noriega's drug trafficking, gun running, money laundering and spying. North Carolina Senator Jesse Helms intensified the debate when he used the Senate Foreign Relations Committee to unravel and publicize Noriega's activities. When Noriega claimed that such attacks were a disguised effort to abrogate the 1979 canal treaties, Washington officials drew sides. The Reagan White House was embarrassed by the situation and wanted to see him go. So too, did the State and Justice Departments, but the Drug Enforcement Agency (DEA), Defense Department and the CIA wanted to continue their relationship with him since he still was able to serve their interests.

In 1987, as Noriega brutally suppressed his political opposition, the U.S. Congress passed resolutions demanding that he hold elections and implement a constitutional and civilian government. When Noriega's gangs attacked the U.S. embassy, consulate and information service buildings, the White House orchestrated secret discussions to pave the way for Noriega's departure and the holding of presidential elections. With the encouragement of Assistant Secretary of State Elliot Abrams, Eric Arturo Delvalle tried to fire Noriega as PDF commander, but Noriega removed the president! The United States then unsuccessfully searched for potential coup leaders in Panama. Hoping to isolate Noriega as an international outlaw, the U.S.

Justice Department filed a series of indictments against Noriega in Miami and Tampa, Florida, for his drug trafficking and money laundering. The administration also attempted the economic strangulation of Panama, first by eliminating the Panamanian sugar quota and closing AID offices and then by cutting off Panama's canal payments, ceasing to remit canal employees taxes and social security contributions, suspending trade preferences, freezing Panamanian assets in the U.S., holding up international bank transfers, barring U.S. companies in Panama from paying local taxes and stopping the shipment of dollars to Panama, which still used U.S. dollars as its national currency. The confiscated funds were put in escrow accounts and by the end of 1989 totalled $110 million. All of Washington's actions were motivated by the upcoming 1988 U.S. presidential election. The incumbent party had two primary concerns regarding Panama: (1) the need to have an acceptable Panamanian assume the canal's chief administrative post in 1990 to insure the continued smooth operation of the canal and (2) the fear that Noriega possessed documents that demonstrated at least some U.S. complicity in his drug, money laundering and arms dealing activities.

But Noriega successfully withstood the U.S. pressure and in January 1989 he became George Bush's problem. Noriega's cancellation of the May 1989 presidential vote counting and subsequent bloodshed beamed across the United States by television and in September his appointment of personal friend, Francisco Rodríguez as provisional president only increased Bush's determination to oust the dictator. Bush continued Reagan's economic sanctions and, as he began his own "war on drugs" in the fall of 1989 and needed a visible scapegoat sent an additional 1,900 troops to the canal zone as a warning to Noriega. It was also getting closer to January 1990, when a Panamanian was to become administrator of the Panama Canal, causing Bush concern over Noriega's intentions regarding the waterway. The stage was being set for a confrontation between Noriega and the United States.

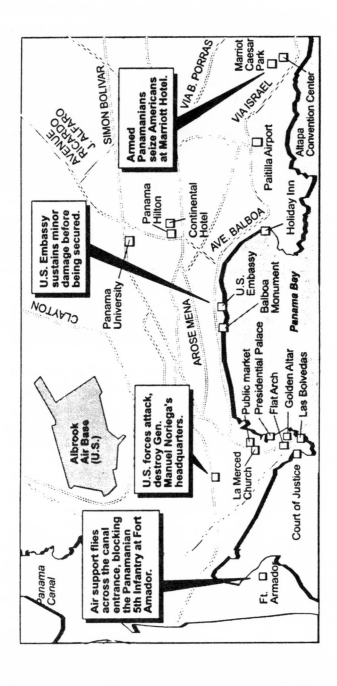

COMING FULL CIRCLE:
THE 1989 INVASION AND AFTER

President George Bush told the American public that in the early morning of December 20, 1989, some 24,000 U.S. troops had invaded Panama "to safeguard the lives of Americans, to defend democracy in Panama, to combat drug trafficking and to protect the integrity of the Panama Canal Treaties." Within an hour of the invasion a civilian government under President Guillermo Endara had been installed and the United States government released some Panamanian assets that had been held in escrow and lifted economic sanctions that had been imposed in 1986.

Bush's explanation, however, may have ignored other motivations. Since the Panamanians and North Americans allegedly instigated incidents, the safeguarding lives could have been handled without an invasion. Given Panama's tortured political history, one can question if the nation ever experienced democracy. And if the North Americans were going to combat drug trafficking in Panama with military force, other regional countries could have easily been targeted. Instead, an examination of United States post-invasion actions in Panama indicate that Bush gave a broad interpretation to the meaning of the "integrity of the Panama Canal Treaties." With the destruction of the Panamanian Defense Forces, the republic was no longer capable of meeting the requirement that it defend the canal after the year 2000. This opened the door to the possible abrogation of the 1977 treaties and with the it the U.S. right to maintain its military bases in Panama and defend the canal well into the future.

In the 86 years since 1903 when Panama achieved its independence, both Panamanian political dynamics and United States foreign policy had come full circle. In 1903, Panama's political leadership was frustrated by the dictates of the central government at Bogotá, while in 1989 the civilian political leadership was discontent with the dictates of Manuel Noriega. In 1903, the United States wanted a transisthmian canal secure from foreign intervention and regional political instability. In December 1989, the United States did not anticipate a politically stable future for Panama which would enable the republic to defend the canal when it passed into its possession. In both instances, the United States found a political leader that served its interests.

LIBERATING PANAMA: THE DECEMBER 1989 INVASION

By 1986, when Noreiga no longer served U.S. interests, the Reagan administration determined to oust Manuel Noriega from power in Panama, but his increasingly brutal and repressive regime, alone, was not sufficient reason to intervene. However, when the U.S. Congress moved to eliminate the administration's covert aid to the Nicaraguan contras, Noriega no longer served as a valuable ally. In 1988, when President George Bush made the "war on drugs" a centerpiece of his domestic and foreign policy, the drug trafficking Noriega became even less tolerable. Still, by the time of the May 1989 Panamanian presidential elections, the U.S. diplomatic and economic sanctions had failed to dislodge the dictator. On the surface, Bush's response to Noriega's brutality following those elections appeared as if the president could do more than express his frustration. He recalled Ambassador Arthur Davis, ordered U.S. government employees and dependents relocated out of Panama or into the Canal Zone, announced the continuation of economic sanctions against Panama and proclaimed that the United States would cooperate with the Organization of American States (OAS) in trying to mediate Panama's political crisis.

Below the surface, however, Bush did more than stay the course. Publically, Bush encouraged the Panamanian Defense Forces to play an important role in establishing a democratic future in the republic by pointing to their constitutional obligation to defend democracy. He reaffirmed the United States 1977 treaty right to increase the number of U.S. troops in Panama by dispatching a brigade size force to the isthmus to augment the troops already there. Privately, he instructed the Pentagon to review existing military plans for operations in Panama. The thought of apprehending Noriega in Panama for trial in the United States was reinforced when the Justice Department issued an opinion on June 21, 1989 that granted the president legal authority to direct the Federal Bureau of Investigation (FBI) to abduct a fugitive residing in a foreign country for violation of United States law, even if the arrest was contrary to customary international law. Throughout the summer of 1989, while Washington was laying the groundwork for a still undefined action, tensions in Panama increased as Noriega stepped up the brutality against his opposition and U.S. forces confronted the PDF as they carried out exercises within the republic.

Events in Panama on the weekend of September 29 to October 1, 1989 gave the Bush administration its first opportunity to move against Noriega. On Saturday the 30th, General Maxwell Thurman took command of SOUTHCOM in the Canal Zone. Thurman was within months of ending a 36 year career, having risen to the rank of four star general, but never having had a high visibility post. He soon would. At midnight October 1, General Colin Powell took over as Chairman of the Joint Chiefs of Staff. At age 53, Powell was the youngest chairman in history and the first black to hold the post. He had served as National Security Advisor late in the Reagan administration, where he impressed then Vice President Bush with his knowledge of world affairs and his sense of energy.

About two a.m. on the morning of October 1, before the command changes were complete, Thurman learned from two CIA agents in Panama that PDF Major Moisés Giroldi wanted U.S. assistance in an effort to oust Noriega. Only eighteen months earlier, in March 1988, Giroldi played a major role in helping Noriega to crush a PDF coup attempt against its commander-in-chief. Now, Giroldi was convinced that he and 200 lower ranking officers could talk Noriega and his senior ranking officers into retirement. Giroldi wanted U.S. forces to block major roads into Panama City in order to prevent troops loyal to Noriega from interfering with the planned coup and for SOUTHCOM to provide sanctuary for his wife and children. Thurman relayed the information to Washington with the recommendation that the United States distance itself from this absurd plan. In Washington, Powell and Secretrary of Defense Richard Cheney concurred with Thurman, although Cheney agreed to provide sanctuary for Giroldi's family. The secretary made no verbal committment on the use of U.S. troops to block roads.

The coup went badly from the start. The original nine a.m. starting time was delayed until the afternoon of October 1 and then until the next day. When it got underway on the morning of October 2, Noriega was already at the Comandancía. Although Cheney had given no public assurances, when asked by the press, he subsequently used the 1977 canal treaties as justification for U.S. troops to conduct routine training along the roads that led to Fort Amador and Howard Air Force Base and, in so doing, effectively blockaded the PDF in those areas from reaching the capital city. But the U.S. did not have rights or a plausibly deniable excuse for holding exercises along the road to Tucoman airport, thus leaving the path open to Major Francsico Olechea to bring loyal troops to Noriega's rescue. In the defeat of the coup on October 3, at least ten people lost their lives, including Giroldi, and 77 junior officers who supported the coup were immediately jailed.

For two weeks after the failed coup, the Bush administration was admonished by the Democrats in Congress and the media.

One group of critics that pointed to Bush's statements encouraging the PDF to act charged that when it did, the administration should have been ready and willing to use force to support the rebels. These critics wanted to know if the administration had contingency plans for such an occurance and why the National Security Council (NSC) apparently failed to coordinate intelligence and devise an appropriate response. The second group of critics chastized the administration for not accepting Giroldi and the younger officers as a viable alternative to Noriega. After all, given Panama's political history and the military role in government since the Remón era, a civilian government did not appear as an option. In sum, both groups faulted the lack of preparedness and the decision making at the highest levels of government.

In Panama, the disheartened opposition was equally critical of the United States for not taking stronger action, especially after sending opposite signals beforehand. Noriega, exhilirated by his success, used the coup attempt to purge the PDF of suspected disloyalists and to reorganize the officer corps to reward less experienced but more loyal men. The confident Noriega boasted to government employees on October 6 that he had "bullets for his enemy, beatings for the indecisive and money for his friends." He also announced sixteen laws designed to identify and punish dissenters. Noriega appeared to be in firm control.

Surprised by the events in Panama and stung by the critics at home, Bush ordered an immediate policy review from which emerged a consensus that the United States must have military options in place because the existing policy of supporting a Panamanian coup was no longer viable. As a result, SOUTHCOM commander, General Maxwell Thurman, designed a plan that provided for an overnight invasion designed to seize Noriega, destroy the PDF and prepare the way for the restoration of democracy. While Thurman planned, an Army Judge Advocate's ruling legalized military operations against terrorists, drug lords or fugitives from U.S. law abroad. In early November, "readiness" exercises were held in the United States and Panama and tanks and helicopters were prepositioned at U.S. defense sites in the republic. By early December, the U.S. was prepared to exercise the military option and also to apprehend Noriega. It only awaited an opportunity to act.

The opportunity came the weekend of December 15. On that day, Noriega had the National Assembly name him "Maximum Leader," the title held by Torrijos from 1972 to 1978. Noriega also received the power to appoint government officials, direct foreign affairs and convene the Council of State, the cabinet and the assembly. These legislative actions legalized functions that Noriega had previously performed behind the scenes. The Assembly also passed a declaration stating that Panama was "in a state of war so long as the United States continues its policy of aggression," because of continued U.S. psychological and military harrassment against the republic and its citizens.

The atmosphere intensified after the fatal shooting of U.S. Marine Lieutenant Robert Paz by Panamanian forces on December 16 and the detainment and harrassment of Navy Lieutenant Adam J. Curtis and his wife Bonnie on December 17. Paz was killed by gunfire as he and three other U.S. military personnel ran a PDF checkpoint near the Comandancía. Returning from dinner about 9PM, their car was in line at the checkpoint when civilians and the military began shouting anti-American slogans. When the Panamanians acted to remove the North Americans from the car, the driver sped off amidst a haze of bullets, one of which struck Paz. The Curtises witnessed the incident from a nearby street corner from which they were taken by Panamanian forces to a PDF facility where they were detained, blindfolded, and held until the next afternoon. During the detainment, Lt. Curtis was physically abused and his wife subjected to sexual harrassment.

Although these events fit a two year pattern of ever increasing tension, military analysts in Washington concluded that the latest incidents indicated that Noriega had lost control of his personnel because they believed that Noriega understood that the death of any North American would bring some type of reprisal. The decision to act came on the afternoon of December

17, when Bush gathered his advisers at the White House, where they concluded that the situation in Panama could only worsen. After reviewing the details of the military operation for one and one half hours, Bush gave the go ahead orders to remove Noriega and put Endara in the presidential palace.

The invasion, named *Operation Just Cause*, was not a complete surprise. On the afternoon of December 19, Panama protested the violation of its airspace by U.S. planes and helicopters ferrying troops into the Canal Zone. U.S. troops could be seen busying around tanks at Ft. Amador. The NBC Evening News program showed transport planes leaving Ft. Bragg, the home of the 82nd Airborne Division. Later that evening, Noriega reportedly dismissed a report that two of his officers overheard U.S. soldiers stating that one a.m. was the strike hour. Instead, Noriega went off to a motel for a sexual tryst. Some his advisers took the warning more seriously and ordered the PDF to prepare for a U.S. invasion.

As battle plans were readied, Guillermo Endara prepared for dinner. "El Gordo," as the 54 year old obese lawyer is known by his countrymen, had been invited along with Ricardo Arias Calderón and Guillermo Ford to a late night dinner by John Bushnell, the de facto head of the U.S. diplomatic mission. Instead of dinner they learned of the invasion. In a private home forty-five minutes before the invasion began, Endara and the two vice presidents, Arias Calderón and Ford were sworn into office by the head of the Panamanian Commission on Human Rights. At about the same time, for the first time in its history, the Panama Canal was closed for security reasons. It reopened December 21. The invasion began at 1:35 a.m..

Although the worst of the fighting was over within eighteen hours, the conflict lasted nearly a week, because Noriega's "Dignity Battalions" continued to resist and general chaos wracked the streets of Panama City amid widespread looting and violence. By December 24, four top PDF commanders and their troops had surrendered, including Noriega loyalist, Colonel Luis del Cid, who had been indicted with Noriega on drug trafficking charges in the United States. He was turned over to DEA agents and flown to Miami. Noriega, however, escaped his captors for five days. Instead of seeking refuge in the embassy of a friendly country, such as Cuba, Nicaragua or Spain and hoping for safe exile, Noriega turned himself into the Papal Nuncio on Christmas Eve. For the next ten days, Noriega remained inside the Nunciature while U.S. troops surrounded the building and blared rock music and Panamanians held noisy, jublient demonstrations. In the end, Noriega apparently decided that it was better to face trial in the United States on drug charges than to face criminal charges in Panama. On January 4, 1990, he turned himself over to U.S. authorities, who quickly had him flown to Miami where he was jailed.

The official U.S. casualty count was lower than projected: 23 military and three civilian personnel died and another 323 military personnel were wounded. The Panamanian figures caused greater controversy. The United States counted 314 Panamanian soldiers killed and 124 wounded and placed civilian casualties between 500 and 1,000. Local authorities and subsequent investigations by human rights organizations placed the number of civilians killed closer to 2,500. Property damage was estimated to be in the millions and a multitude of private businesses were destroyed in the looting and street fighting that followed the invasion. Hardest hit was the El Chorillo section of Panama City, closest to the Comandencía and home to the poorest Panamanians.

The Defense Department put the cost of the invasion at $163.6 million and Bush explained that it was well spent in the protection of U.S. lives, the defense of Panamanian democracy, the combating of drug trafficking and the protection of the Panama Canal. The State Department explained that the invasion was justified under Article 51 of the United Nations Charter which permits the use of force for self defense. Reaction in the United States was generally favorable, although criticism focused on the high civilian casualties and the destruction of El Chorrillo. The capture of Noriega suggested that the administration intended to get tough on drugs. For this, most Americans were happy.

But the Latin American states were not pleased with the interventionist policy and the Organization of American States (OAS) passed a resoluton deploring the invasion. Peru went further, severing diplomatic relations with Washington. At the United Nations, the United States, Great Britain and France vetoed a Soviet and Chinese Security Council resolution that condemned the invasion and called for the withdrawal of U.S. troops from Panama. The United States, however, could not prevent the passage of a resolution in the General Assembly which chastized the U.S. for violating international law and called for the immediate withdrawal of its troops from the republic.

President Endara dismissed the condemnations, asserting that the return to democracy and the prinicple of self determination justified the use of force. For the moment, the majority of Panamanians agreed with him. But a public opinion poll in early January 1990 indicated that if the U.S. troops stayed in Panama beyond the announced six month period, they would not be welcome. In that brief time period, Bush and Endara had to establish a functioning democracy, reconstruct the economy, repair the war damage and dismantle the PDF.

COMING FULL CIRCLE: THE UNITED STATES AND PANAMA SINCE 1989

For 21 months following his apprehension in Panama, Manuel Noriega resided in a Miami federal detention center while his defense lawyers unsuccessfully argued for his release on the grounds that he was a prisoner of war, having been the victim of an invading power. When that failed, his lawyers unsuccessfully fought for the release of United States government documents that allegedly showed him as an employee of the Central Intelligence and the Drug Enforcement Agencies. With the preliminary maneuvering over, Noriega's trial began in September 1991 and a verdict was finally rendered on April 10, 1992. During the nearly eight months of trial testimony, the U.S. government called more than sixty witnesses, many of them from an international rogues' gallery of drug traffickers and money launderers. In the end, the jury was convinced that the criminals on the witness stand told the truth about the criminal at the defense table and found Noriega guilty on eight of ten charges for drug manufacturing, trafficking drugs into the United States and money laundering. After being sentenced to forty years in prison on July 10, 1992, with the earliest possible release to come when he is 83 years of age, Noriega took three hours in the Miami courtroom to condemn the United States and George Bush for toppling his regime so the United States could take permanent control of the Panama Canal, and he warned that there would be no canal in the year 2000. In Washington, President Bush ignored Noriega's harangue and described the punishment as a message to international drug traffickers. In Panama City, residents honked horns and banged pots in raucous celebration and the government delcared an end to a pitiful chapter in Panama's history. The episode may have registered a victory for George Bush's "war on drugs" and freed Panama of a dictator, but it did not guarantee an end to drug trafficking nor the restoration of the republic to democracy.

Building a democracy in Panama required the construction of institutions lacking in Panamanian history—a functioning legislature, an independent judiciary, viable political parties and competitive free enterprise. The path to democracy began on December 27, 1989, seven days after the American invasion, when the Panamanian Electoral Tribunal validated the May 1989 election results, thus legalizing the Endara government. Furthermore, of the 67 legislative seats, the Tribunal awarded 51 to the Democratic Opposition Civil Alliance (ADOC) that had opposed Noriega, seven seats to the Revolutionary Democratic Party (PRD) that served as Noriega's political arm and declared that the remaining nine seats would be filled by a future election.

Although Endara and his Vice Presidents Arias Calderón and Guillermo Ford took office behind North American guns, optimists pointed to two advantages: (1) that as clear winners of the May 1989 election, they had political and moral mandates beyond doubt and (2) that they were moderate, intelligent and honest men with untainted political images. In contrast, critics pointed out that the Endara coalition had no governing experience and that it represented the white upper class businessmen who had never reached out to the majority of the poor, dark skinned Panamanians, leaving them as a volatile constituency for another populist dictator in the style of Omar Torrijos.

Marred by infighting that often found its way on to the television screen and on the front pages of the press, Endara's coalition splintered in April 1991 when Vice President Arias Calderón withdrew his PDC from the coalition. The PDC was the most popular party, prompting Arias Calderón to demand that it hold more cabinet posts and that its social programs be given greater attention in the legislative assembly. Endara refused and purged his cabinet of PDC members and dismissed Christian Democrats from other government posts. The PDC's departure from ADOC also weakened Endara's hold over the National Assembly.

One cannot attribute the political infighting as the sole cause of Panama'a problems. When Endara assumed the presidency in December 1991, he also inherited an economy in shambles. The Gross Domestic Product had declined by well over 25 percent since 1988. Sugar exports declined by 94 percent, construction by 93 percent and the international banking sector, with over 7,000 quality jobs, became nearly non-existent. Unemployment was estimated at 35 percent of the work force. The government also faced a $6 billion foreign debt and $2 billion in damages caused by the U.S. invasion. Economists estimated that a minimum of $1 billion was needed in the short term and another $2 to 3 billion over three to five years to resurrect the prostrate economy.

Endara, a neo-populist in the Arnulfo Arias tradition, favored state involvement in economic and social issues, but he permitted Vice President Ford free rein to develop free market policies in hopes of attracting United States assistance. Ford immediately announced that international banking could resume without restriction and that the names of depositors and account numbers would remain secret. Other government economists worked on programs to guarantee the safety of foreign investment and to encourage development of Panama's interior, both to diversify the economy and to ease the social services strain on the capital. There also was a plea for a huge public works project, including homes, shops and public offices in the slum area of Panama City's El Chorillo district that had born the brunt of the U.S. invasion.

As the Endara administration struggled with economic development plans, it faced a serious international debt problem. In September 1990 a team from the World Bank and the Inter-American Development Bank visited the republic to discuss structural reforms that included the privatization of many government owned industries. Although Panama met its 1990 debt service by non-traditional sources that included the release of $278.4 million in frozen U.S. funds, no such sources were expected for 1991 to pay the service on Panama's $6.21 billion in external and internal debt, estimated to be $400.8 million or 49 percent of the anticipated ordinary government income. To address the problem, the World Bank recommended in April 1991 that the government lay off 19,000 of its 150,000 employees, privatize eleven state run industries and cut minimum wages by 10 percent in order to normalize relations with its creditors. Without an alternative, Endara succumbed in August. The layoffs were estimated to provide the Panamanian government $24 million in 1992 and $46 million in 1993 just to pay its foreign debt. By July 1992, the Panamanian government had disposed of seven state run industries including Air Panama, the Atlantic Banana Corporation, Chiriqui Citrus Company, the Ancon District Bus Service and the management of a tourist beach on the canal.

Given the historical relationship between the United States and Panama and the economic sanctions in place since 1986, one would think that the Bush administration would have had post invasion economic plans in place. It did not, but within a week of the invasion, Deputy Secretary of State Lawrence Eagleburger led a team of administration officials to Panama to show visible concern for rebuilding the republic and bolster Endara's image. Before 1989 was over, the U.S. government began the process of unblocking $70 million in Panamanian funds and lifted trade restrictions. Despite these gestures, Assistant Secretary of State for Latin American Affairs Bernard Aronson signalled the Bush administration's attitude in July 1990, when he observed that while the social and economic problems confronting the Panamanians were enormous, its government must break the mental habit of looking to the United States to solve its problems. Most Panamanians disagreed with Aronson. Admittedly they were free of a despot, but the United States bore responsibilty for the economic damage inflicted upon Panama because of Noriega's regime.

On January 25, 1990, Bush asked Congress for $1 billion in reconstruction aid for Panama. Later he scaled the request back to $500 milliion. More than one recalcitrant congressman pointed out that there were increased pressures for aid to Eastern Europe, Israel, Egypt and El Salvador. Except for a $42 million aid package in February, Congress was slow to act. Many congressmen wanted to link aid to reforms in the Panamanian banking system so that it no longer served as a money launderer. When Congress finally approved a scaled down $420 million assistance package in May 1990, it did so with strings attached. Congress insisted upon a Mutual Legal Assistance Treaty that opened Panamanian bank records to U.S. officials in order to track drug traffickers and money launderers. Under pressure from local bankers, Endara resisted signing the agreement until April 1992. The agreement opened the door to the aid package passed the preceding year, but also led to charges of violations of Panamanian sovereignty.

By the end of 1990, Ford's free market approach had resulted in $804 million in new deposits in Panama's international banks and 90 percent of the looted businesses reopened. By mid-1992, Panama's annual economic growth rate was at a hemispheric high of 9.3%. Clothing boutiques, bankers, shippers, merchants and builders all reported record sales. Luxury high rise condominimums, selling for upwards to

$400,000, appeared in Panama City. But critics such as University of Panama economics Professor Juan Jovane charged that Panama's economic development was lagging because the government agreed to meet its foreign debt payments at the expense of investments in health, housing and education.

There was much evidence to support Jovane's position. Although the unemployment rate steadily declined following the 1989 invasion, it stood at 25 percent in Panama City and fifty percent in Colón and nearly half of Panama's 2.4 million people lived below the poverty level at the end of 1992. The poverty was most evident in El Chorrillo, which had been destroyed in the invasion and not yet rebuilt. In December 1992, some 4,500 of its former residents were still housed in airplane hangers at the U.S. Albrook Air Base. The government made no effort to address the income gap and, in fact, proposed a revision of the Labor Code to lessen wage demands.

The economic and social disparities played out in increased demonstrations and violence directed at the Endara administration and subsequently the United States. The government recorded a 300 percent increase in crime in 1991 over 1990. A wave of new private security companies were organized by former members of the PDF. A pro-Noriega group, the Movement of the 20th of December (M-20), claimed responsibility for the killing of several government officials, private businessmen and at least one U.S. soldier. The U.S. Drug Enforcement Agency reported in 1992 that drug use and trafficking increased dramatically after Noriega's ouster.

Critics warned that if the government did not soon correct the social imbalance, it would face an explosive situation. Vice President Ford understood this too. In February 1992, he announced that for the first time in five years, Panama was able to borrow money for a job creating public works program, because it had paid its international lenders $645.8 million.

The tension climaxed on June 11, 1992, when President Bush planned a six hour stop over in Panama enroute to the Earth Summit Conference in Rio de Janerio, Brazil. Many Panaminans wanted to capitalize upon his visit to express their discontent with the level of U.S. post invasion economic assistance. Included were businessmen who lost millions of dollars in the looting that followed the invasion in Panama City and Colón and residents of El Chorillo who were disatisfied with the offer of $6,500 for new homes. For others, it was the continued presence of U.S. troops in Panama, seen as a violation of the 1977 treaties. Bush's visit was short lived. Panamanian police broke up a crowd of 200 rock throwing demonstrators that allegedly threatened Bush and Endara as they prepared to address a friendly crowd in Panama City. Critics focused on the over reaction of the Panamanian police, but an analysis of television tapes showed that a number of anti-Endara people were in the crowd, including Balbina Herrera, a PRD legislator, and Cleto Sousa, the leader of Panama's left wing People's Party.

The economic and social issues overshadowed the fate of the Panamanian Defense Forces. Its elimination had been a primary objective of the U.S. invasion and President Endara echoed this commitment during his first trip abroad in January 1990, to Costa Rica, where he declared that Panama would no longer have an army. Subsequently, a National Police force, loyal to the government, was established. The Air Force and the Navy were renamed the National Air Sevice and National Naval Service. Denied combat training, they were to perform only transport services. Former PDF responsibilities for immigration and prison supervision were assigned to civilians. The legal basis of the police force's subordinate role to the government came in June 1991 with a proposed constitutional amendment stating that the republic would no longer have an army. The Panamanian people rejected the proposed amendment in a November 1992 referendum.

The dissolution of the PDF and the establishment of a National Police, however, did not solve security problems. Many Panamanians came to view the police as a continuation of the PDF minus 410 pro-Noriega officers. Others questioned its loyalty to the civilian government, citing its links to the M-20 guerrilla group, the coup plots of former commander Colonel Eduardo Herrera and increased reports of graft, corruption and alleged ties to Colombian drug traffickers. Many of these problems were attributed to poor pay, inadequate equipment and supplies, low morale and high turnover in leadership positions. To correct these deficiencies and to make the National Police Force more effective, in 1992 the United States committed $13.2 million as part of an expected $60 million five year program to equip and train Panama's police force.

The inability of the National Police to deal with crime, guerrilla activities and drugs led to the increased presence of United States troops in Panama to detect guerrilla activity and to conduct the "war on drugs." During a May 1992 visit to Washington, Endara initialed three agreements which allowed U.S. soldiers to board vessels bearing the Panamanian flag, to permit U.S. vessels to enter Panamanian territorial waters under specified circumstances and to manage the regulation of chemicals that are used in cocaine manufacturing. Middle sector spokesmen asserted that these actions were a violation of Panamanian sovereignty and increased the republic's dependence upon the United States.

Others asserted that Noriega's removal was only a cover for the United States to reassert its authority over the canal's defense and that the abolishment of a national army was a violation of the 1977 treaties because it rendered Panama incapable of upholding its defense obligations after the year 2000. Although the United States Senate followed the requirements of the 1977 treaties in September 1990 when it approved Gilberto Guardia Fabrega as the first Panamanian administrator of the Panama Canal Commission, Panamanian fears were not assuaged. President Endara and Foreign Minister Julio Linares continually declared that they would never sign any treaty that permitted U.S. military presence in Panama after the year 2000. The canal defense issue also became entwined with Panama's internal problems. In July 1989, Deputy Leo González led a legislative delegation to Washington to discuss the canal's defense beyond 2000, recognizing that without an army and with a weak economy, Panama was in no position to do so. He suggested renegotiating the treaties. At the same time, a group of Panamanian lawyers came forward to suggest that the government pay greater attention to the republic's internal problems, rather than concern itself with the canal's defense. They pointed out that the canal was not secure from either missiles or sabotage, so the issue was moot. A poll in June 1992, showed that more than 70 percent of the Panamanian population wanted the U.S. to maintain its defense sites beyond the year 2000, largely because some 12,000 civilian jobs would be lost with their closing.

The United States also signalled its intention to continue defending the canal. The joint United States-Panamanian Committee to provide for defense cooperation between the PDF and SOUTHCOM has not met since December 1989. Ambassador Dean Hinton asserted that there was no need for it to meet. In the summer of 1991, a group of fourteen U.S. Republican party Senators, who shared González's opinion, suggested that the defense provisions of the 1977 treaties be restructured. When Bush visited Panama in June 1992, the United States still had 13,000 troops on six bases in Panama, carried out maneuvers in Panama's isolated rugged interior, denied Panamanians access to the modernized Howard Air Force Base and had commenced construction of a military complex in central Panama. In reality, the United States continued to act as if it were sovereign regarding the canal's defense. Those supporting a continuance of the U.S. presence asserted that a demilitarized Panama cannot control internal disorder and subversion, nor could it repel an external attack.

Foreign Minister Linares repeatedly protested the continued presence of U.S. troops in the republic as a violation of the 1977 treaties and asserted that they could leave their defense sites only with Panamanian authorization. In Washington, administration spokesmen countercharged that only the U.S. President and Congress can determine what actions are necessary for Canal Zone security. Thus, when George Bush visited the country in June 1992, Linares protested the presence of U.S. troops and armored personnel carriers on the streets of Panama City, a protest dismissed by Ambassador Hinton as a Panamanian misunderstanding of the 1977 treaties. After Bush's departure, the presence in Panama of out-of-uniform U.S. military personnel and their armored vehicles increased, leaving Washington's intentions to speculation. A creative way out of the crisis has been proposed by former Costa Rican President Oscar Arias who suggested that the United Nations supervise the waterway. While this suggestion fell on deaf ears in both Panama City and Washington, the question will reach another highwater mark in mid 1993, when a joint United States-Panamanian commission, appointed in 1985, makes its recommendation on whether to expand the current canal or replace it with a new one.

There is a consistent pattern in Panama's history and its relations with the United States. Even before independence in 1903, a white commercial elite wanted political power for itself and, after achieving it in 1903, has sought to maintain that position at the expense of its rural counterpart, the middle sector, the military, the Panamanian poor and the West Indians and their descendents. Over the years, the white commercial elite lost its pre-eminent position, only to reclaim it in 1989 with United States assistance, just as it had obtained it in 1903. But Panama's political landscape had appreciably changed in the intervening 86 years. The other political actors, with the exception of the West Indians and their descendents, had participated in Panama's political arena and for the elite to think that they can now be excluded is sheer folly.

Historically, the United States preferred to deal with Panama's white commercial elite because it wanted little more than some semblance of shared sovereignty over the Canal Zone. In that respect, Guillermo Endara today is little different than Manuel Amador in 1903. Panama's white commercial elite resisted political participation from representatives of the middle sector, the military and the poor—Arnulfo Arias, José Remón and Omar Torrijos—and over the years the United States did not encourage or support their political participation. Officials in Washington consistently thought that they could be bought off with economic concessions, while maintaining U.S. sovereignty over the Canal Zone. The post 1989 invasion policy is in that tradition.

Manuel Noriega had become an anathema to both. His obsession for power and abuse of Panamanian society threatened not only the republic's established economic, social and political structures, but also the very operation of the Panama Canal and, with it, United States vital commercial and defense interests. The same vital interests that prompted Teddy Roosevelt to act in 1903 prompted George Bush to act in 1989. Panama's political history and U.S. foreign policy had come full circle.

CHART ONE

United States Economic & Military Assistance to Panama

Presidential Administration	Economic Aid	Military Aid
Harry S. Truman (1945-1952)	$ 3.0	-----
Dwight D. Eisenhower (1953-1960)	54.9	$ 0.1
John F. Kennedy & Lyndon Johnson (1961-1968)	290.2	3.0
Richard M. Nixon & Gerald R. Ford (1969-1976)	152.1	5.9
Jimmy Carter (1977-1980)	56.9	2.6
Ronald R. Reagan (1981-1988)	154.6	41.5
George W. Bush (1989-1992)	*469.7**	-----
TOTALS	$1,181.4	$53.1

Source: Agency for International Development, *U.S. Overseas Loans & Grants and Assistance for International Organizations* (Washington, D.C.) Annual 1962 to 1990. Figures for George W. Bush Presidency provided verbally by the Agency for International Development Office, Washington.

* Includes $27.78 million estimate for 1992.

BIBLIOGRAPHICAL ESSAY

The bibliographical essay focuses upon the most salient literature in each of the three topics covered in the text: The Panama Canal, Panamanian history and United States-Panamanian relations. While it provides a framework for understanding each topic, those wishing to go beyond these sources, should consult Wayne Bray's annotated guide, *The Controversy Over a New Canal Treaty Between the United States and Panama* (Washington, D. C.: Government Printing Office, 1976). Another important reference, in which English language sources dominate, is Eleanor Langstaff, *Panama* (Santa Barbara, Cal.: ABC-CLIO, 1982). For Spanish language sources see Carlos Manuel Gasteazoro et. al., *La historia de Panamá en sus textos* (Panama City: Universidad de Panamá, 1980) Volume 2, 331-448. An introduction to the literature on United States relations with Panama can be found in Richard Dean Burns ed. *A Guide to American Foreign Relations Since 1700* (Santa Barbara, Cal.: ABC-CLIO, 1983).

THE PANAMA CANAL

A good beginning point on the history of transisthmian canal projects are Gerstle Mack's *The Land Divided: A History of the Panama Canal and Other Isthmian Projects* (New York: Knopf, 1944) and David Howarth's *Panama: 400 Years of Dreams and Cruelty* (New York: McGraw Hill, 1966). Some earlier important studies include I. E. Bennett, *History of the Panama Canal* (Washington, D. C.: The Historical Publishing Company, 1915) and Willis F. Johnson, *Four Centuries of the Panama Canal* (New York: Henry Holt, 1906).

For technical studies of the various canal sites see: United States Congress, Senate, Report of the Commission Appointed by the President March 15, 1872, Relating to the Different Interoceanic Canal Surveys and the Practicability of the Construction of a Ship-Canal Across the Continent, 46th Congress, 1st sess., Sen. Exec. Doc No. 15 (Washington, D. C.: Government Printing Office, 1879) and Report of the Isthmian Canal Commission, 1899-1901, 58th Cong. 2nd sess., Sen. Doc. No. 222 (Washington, D. C.: Government Printing Office, 1904). The latter is popularly known as the "Walker Commission" Report.

There were several efforts to traverse the isthmus in the nineteenth century. A dated, but still important study is John H. Kemble's *The Panama Route, 1848-1869* (Berkeley: University of California, 1943). A good description of the French canal effort can be found in Maron J. Simon, *The Panama Affair* (New York: Charles Scribner's Sons, 1971)

Phillipe Bunau-Varilla detailed the French interests in his *Panama: The Creation, Destruction and Resurrection* (New York: Robert McBride, 1920). A recent important contribution is James M. Skinner, *France and Panama: The Unknown Years, 1894-1898* (New York: P. Lang, 1989) which discusses the machinations of the New French Panama Canal Company. The story of the Panama railroad is found in R. Hebard, *The Panama Railroad: The First Transcontinental Railroad, 1855-1955* (New York: The MacMillan Company, 1955).

The canal's construction is discussed in William L. Sibert and John F. Stevens, *The Construction of the Panama Canal* (New York: D. A. Appleton, 1915) and George W. Goethals (comp.), *The Panama Canal*, 2 volumes (New York: McGraw Hill, 1916). A description of the canal zone administration is United States Army, *History of the Panama Canal Department*, 4 volumes (Quarry Heights, Panama Canal Zone: Panama Canal Dept., 1947). The best account of the Canal Zone history is John Major, "The Panama Canal Zone, 1904-1979", in Leslie Bethal ed., *Cambridge History of Latin America*, volume 7, (Cambridge, Eng.: Cambridge University Press, 1990), 643-670. The tension that developed between Panamanians and Zonians was captured by Harry A. Franck, *Zone Policeman 88,* 2nd ed. (New York: Arno Press, 1970) and by Willis J. Abbot, *The Panama Canal: An Illustrated Historical Narrative* (New York, Syndicate Publishing Company, 1922) for the early years and by Herbert and Mary Knapp, *Red, White and Blue Paradise: The American Canal Zone in Panama* (New York: Harcourt Brace Jovanovich, 1984) for the contemporary period.

PANAMA'S HISTORY AND SOCIETY

Because a contemporary English language historical study of Panama is lacking, a good starting point for those needing a perspective of the republic is Sandra W. Meditz and Dennis M. Hanratty, eds., *Panama: A Country Study* (Washington: Government Printing Office, 1989). A volume in the Area Handbook Studies series, it provides an excellent introduction to the nation's history, politics, society and economy. A brief historical account is Michael Conniff, "Panama Since 1903," in volume 7, Leslie Betha, 1 ed. *Cambridge History of Latin*

America (Cambridge, Eng.: Cambridge University Press, 1990), 603-642. Excellent overviews in Spanish are Enrique J. Arce and Juan B. Sosa's *Compendio de historia de Panama* (Panama: Litho Impresora Panama, 1971) and Ernesto Castillero Reyes, *Historia Panama* (Panama City: Editor Panama América, 1962). The nation's history as seen through the newspaper *Panama's Star and Herald* is told by Jean G. Niemeier in *The Panama Story* (Portland, Ore.: Metropolitan Press, 1968). For the most part, the study of Panamanian political dynamics until 1968 is found in period and topical studies or incorporated into examinations of the republic's relations with the United States noted below.

For the colonial period see Mary W. Holms, *Ancient Panama: Chiefs in Search of Power* (Austin, University of Texas Press, 1979) and Elliot D. C. Ward, *Imperial Panama: Commerce and Conflict in Isthmian America, 1550-1750*, Ph. D. diss, University of Florida, 1988. A social history of the colonial period can be found in Lady Mallet, *Sketches of Spanish Colonial Life in Panama* (New York: Sturgis and Walton, 1951). The independence of Panama and the debate over its linkage to Gran Colombia is examined by Arnold M. Friedman, *The Independence of Panama and Its Incorporation in Gran Colombia, 1820-1830*, M. A. thesis, University of Florida, 1978, and Andrés Araúz, *La independencía de Panama en 1821* (Panama City: Academia Panameña de la Historia, 1980). Among the most important studies of Panama during the nineteenth century are Alex Perez-Venero, *Before the Five Frontiers: Panama from 1821 to 1903* (New York: AMS Press, 1978) Rodrigo Miro, *Nuestros siglo XIX: hombres y aconteceras* (Panama City: Instituto de Investigaciones Historicos, 1990) and Alfredo Figuroa Navaro, *Domino y sociedad en el Panama Colombiano, 1821-1903* (Panama City: Editorial Universataria, 1982).

In the late nineteenth century, the 1886 Colombian constitution and the War of a Thousand Days that significantly contributed to Panama's final steps towards independence have received much attention. Among the most important studies are: German Vincent Jones, *The Colombian Constitution of 1886 and its Political Repercussions in the Department of Panama*, M. A. thesis, Univesity of Florida, 1975) Patricia Pizarro Gelos, *Antecedentes, hechos y consequencias de la Guerra de los Mil Dias en el istmo de Panama* (Panama City: Panama Ediciones Fomento, 1990) and Humberto E. Ricord, *Panama en la Guerra de los Mil Dias* (Panama City: H. C. Ricord, 1989).

Most of the literature dealing with the independence of Panama in 1903 falls within the purview of United States relations with the republic, but there are some studies detailing the Panamanian side. Joseph Arbena, "The Panama Problem in Colombian History," Ph. D. diss., University of Virginia, 1970; Thomas R. Favell, "The

Antecedents of Panama's Separation from Colombia: A Study in Colombian Politics" Ph. D. diss., Fletcher School of Law and Diplomacy, 1950; and Catalino Arrocha Graell, *Historia de la independencia de Panama: sus antecedents y sus causas, 1821-1903* (Panama City: Academia Panameña de la Historia, 1975) best explain the regional dynamics of Colombian-Panamanian relations. A Colombian perspective is presented by Eduardo Román Lemaitre in his *Panama y su separación de Colombia* (Bogotá: Banco Popular, 1972). Juan Cristobal Zuniga C. has made a significant contribution with his study *El general Tomás Herrera* (Panama City: Panama Imp. S., 1986). For Colombia's reaction to the Panamanian revolt see Jospeh Arbena, "Colombian Reactions to the Independence of Panama, 1903-1904," *The Americas* 33 (July 1976), 130-148. By March 1904, a number of Latin American countries had extended recognition to Panama. For a discussion see E. Bradford Burns, "The Recognition of Panama by the Major Latin American States," *The Americas*, 26 (1969-1970), 3-14, and John Patterson, "Latin American Reactions to the Panama Revolution of 1903," *Hispanic American Historical Review* 24 (May, 1944), 342-351.

The struggle between the Liberal and Conservative parties during the canal's construction period (1904-1914) is examined by Gustavo A. Mellander, *The United States in Panamanian Politics: The Intriguing Formative Years* (Danville, Ill.: Interstate Printers and Publishers, 1971). A more critical analysis of the period is Manual M. Valdés. *Las intervenciones electorales en Panama* (Panama City: Star & Herald, 1932). A historical perspective on the Panamanians during this time period is Ruben Darió Carlos, *Reminiscences de los primeros anos de la Republica de Panama, 1903-1912* (Panama City: La Estrella de Panama, 1968).

Studies of Panama's political history after the canal opened through 1968 are scarce, except as they are incorporated into the larger studies of United States relations with Panama. One major exception is Ricuarte Soler, *Panama: nación y oligarquía, 1925-1975* (Panama City: Imprenta Cervantes, 1976). There are important studies which provide insights into particular time periods. Octavio Sisnett's *Belisario Porras o la vocación de la nacionalidad* (Panama City: Universidad de Panama, 1972) provides an overview of politics through the 1920s. José Conte Porras' *Arnulfo Arias Madrid* (Panama City: Conte Porras', 1980) is an excellent analysis of one of Panama's most controversial figures. Thomas M. Leonard's "United States Perception of Panamanian Politics, 1944-1949," *Journal of Third World Studies* 5 (Fall, 1988), 112-138 provides an insight into the political controversy immediately after World War II. Lawrence LaRae Pippin, *The Rémon Era: An Analysis of a Decade of Events in Panama, 1947-1957*

(Stanford: Institute of Hispanic and Luso-Brazilian Studies, 1964) stands alone for understanding the 1950s. Influenced by Fidel Castro's success in Cuba, Jules Dubois in *Danger Over Panama* (Indianopolis: Bobbs-Merrill, 1964) warned that Panama's socio-political disparities provided an excellent opportunity for the communists to seize upon. The 1964 riots which illustrated the strains in Panamanian society were detailed in the International Commission of Jurists, *Report on the Events in Panama, January 9-12, 1964* (Geneva, Switzerland: 1964) and Lyman M. Tondel, et. al., *The Panama Canal: Background Papers and Proceedings of the Sixth Hammarskjold Forum* (New York: The Association of the Bar of the City of New York, 1964).

The most complete analysis of Panamanian society for this time period is John and Mavis Biesanz, *The People of Panama* (New York: Columbia University Press, 1955). There are several important studies of individual social sectors. Richard N. Adams' *Cultural Survey of Panama, Nicaragua, Guatemala, El Salvador, Honduras* (Washington, D. C.: Pocket Books, 1950) is important for its study of the *campesino* in the interior. The Panamanian middle sector during the 1940s was analyzed in essays by John Biesanz, Georgina Jiménez de López, Carolyn Campbell and Ofelía Hooper in Theo R. Crevenna, *Materials para el estudio de la clase media en la America Latina*, Vol. IV (Washington, D. C.: Pan American Union, 1950). An excellent analysis of the student movement in the 1960s in Daniel Goldrich, *Sons of the Establishment: Elite Youth in Panama and Costa Rica* (Chicago: Rand McNally, 1966). A broader perspective can be found in José Conte Porras, *La rebelión de las esfinges: historia del moviemiento estudiantil panemeño* (Panama City: Litho Impresora Panama, 1978). Stephen Gudeman's *Relationships, Residence and the Individual: A Rural Panamanian Community* (Minneapolis: University of Minnesota Press, 1976) provides an excellent description of rural life in Panama. Another excellent study is Gloria R. Frazier, "Moving to Stand Still: The Third World Poverty and Rural-to-Urban Migration-A Panamanian Case Study," Ph. D. diss., University of Pittsburgh, 1976.

Two important studies of the Panamanian labor movement are Manuel Hernando Franco Muñoz, *Movimiento obrero panameño, 1914 -1921* (Panama City: s.i.,s.n., 1979) and Marco A. Gandásegui, et. al., *Las luchas obreras en Panama, 1850-1978* (Panama City: Centro de Estudios Latinoamericanos, 1980). The most complete study of the West Indian population in Panama is Michael Conniff's *Black Labor on a White Canal, 1904-1981* (Pittsburgh: University of Pittsburgh Press, 1985). An excellent analysis of the same subject in the nineteenth century can be found in Lancelot S. Lewis' "The West Indian in Panama: Black Labor in Panama, 1850-1914," Ph. D. diss., Tulane University, 1975. A personal account is George Westerman's *Los inmigrantes antillanos en Panama* (Panama City: Impresora de la Nación, 1980).

Studies of Panama's economic development also are sketchy. A pioneering work for the colonial period is Richard F. Behrendt, "Aspectos sociales y económicos del Istmo de Panama durante la época del tráfico interocenico primitivo, 1519-1848," *Revista mexicana de sociología* 5 (enero, 1943), 4962. Two descriptive works for the nineteenth century are Omar Jaõn Suárez, "Economía panameña en el siglo XIX: la contrabilidad de hacienda pública de 1849-1903," *Anales de ciencías humanas*, 2 (diciembre, 1972), 87-90, and Luis Ng, *Los presupuestos de rentas y gastos de Panama de 1870 a 1903* (Panama City: Universidad de Panama 1972). William C. Merrill's, et. al., *Panama's Economic Development: the Role of Agriculture* (Ames, Iowa: Iowa State University Press, 1975), is the most thorough study of that economic sector during the twentieth century.

A series of British reports provide the best description of Panama's economy before World War II: Constantine M. Graham, *Report on the Commercial and Economic Situation in the Republic of Panama and Costa Rica, 1920* (London: His Majesty's Stationary Office, 1921) Keith R. Jopson, *Report on the Economic, Financial and Commercial Conditions of the Republic of Panama and the Panama Canal Zone* (London: His Majesty's Stationary Office, 1924) Alan D. Francis, *Economic Conditions in the Republic of Panama and the Panama Canal Zone, 1929* (London: His Majesty's Stationary Office, 1930) C. F. W. Andrews, *Report on the Economic and Commercial Conditions in the Republic of Panama and the Panama Canal Zone, 1933-1935* (London: His Majesty's Stationary Office, 1936) and C. F. W. Andrews, *Report on the Economic and Commercial Conditions in the Republic of Panama, 1936-1937* (London: HMSO, 1938).

The first post-war analysis was done by John Beisanz in his "Economy of Panama," *Inter-American Economic Affairs* 6 (Summer, 1952), 3-28, but comprehensive studies of the Panamanian economy after 1945 until the early 1960s remain lacking. An important contribution is A. J. Jaffe, "Economic Growth and the Male Working Force of Panama, 1950-1960," *American Journal of Economics and Sociology*, 25 (July, 1966), 297-306. It reviews the problem of a dwindling job market for an increased Panamanian labor force. Otherwise, only narrowly focused studies are available, including the United States Tariff Commission, *Mining and Manufacturing Industries in Panama* (Washington, Government Printing Office, 1945) Joaquín F. Franco, *La zona libre de Colón o una institución fundamental para la economía panameña* (Colon: Imprenta Hernández, 1958) Charles F. Denton, "Interests Groups in Panama and the Central American Common Market," *Inter-American Economic Affairs, 21*

(Summer, 1967), 49-61, and two analyses of the agricultural sector, "Agrarian Code in Panama," *International Labor Review*, 89 (February, 1964), 181-188, and Robert H. Fuson, "Land Tenure in Central Panama," *Journal of Geography,* 63 (April, 1964), 161-164. Beginning in 1960 the Inter-American Bank's annual *Social and Economic Progress Reports* and the United Nation's Economic Commission for Latin America's annual *Economic Survey of Latin America* include sections on Panama.

The best scholarly analysis of the Torrijos years can be found in Steve C. Ropp, *Panamanian Politics: From Guarded Nation to National Guard* (New York: Praeger Publishers, 1982) and German Muñoz, "Panamanian Political Reality: The Torrijos Years," Ph. D. diss., University of Miami, 1981. A readable popular account, that also includes the Noriega period, is Richard M. Koster and Guillermo Sánchez, *In the Time of the Tyrants* (New York: Norton, 1990). The issues of the 1968 election that led to the Torrijos coup are found in the *Panama Election Factbook: May 12, 1968* (Washington, D. C.: Institute for the Study of Comparative Politics, 1968). Torrijos speaks for himself in *Nuestra revolución* (Panama City: Ministerio de Relaciones Exteriores, 1974). George Priestly, in his *Military Government and Popular Participation in Panama* (Boulder: Westview Press, 1986) and Renato Pereira in *Panama: Fuerzas armadas y politica* (Panama City: Ediciones Nueva Universidad, 1979) examine the role that the military played in Torrijos' socio-economic policies.

There are several topical studies important to understanding the Torrijos' policies. Torrijos' industrial development policy is explained by Simeón E. González H., *Industrialización y producción capitalista en Panama* (Panama City: Centro de Estudios Latinoamericanos, 1977). A critical account of that policy is Marcos A. Gandasegui, "Industrialización e inveriones extranjeras en Panama," *Estudios sociales centroaméricanos*, 7 (enero-abril, 1974), 1-34. Panama's growth as an international banking center is examined in Harry Johnson's "Panama as a Regional Financial Center: A Preliminary Analysis of Development Contribution," *Economic Development and Cultural Change Survey* 24 (January, 1976), 261-286, and in Robin Pringle's, "Panama: A Survey," *The Banker* 125 (October, 1975), 191-210. An excellent analysis of Torrijos' labor policies is made by Sharron Phillips, "Labor Policy in an Inclusionary-Authoritarian Regime: Panama Under Torrijos," Ph. D. diss., University of New Mexico, 1987. An analysis of the inflationary impact of Torrijos' policies is made by Robert E. Looney in *The Economic Development of Panama* (New York: Praeger, 1976).

Manuel Noriega's regime has received much attention. In addition to Koster and Sánchez noted above, early popular accounts include

Frederick Kempe, *Divorcing the Dictator: America's Bungled Affair with Noriega* (New York: G. P. Putnam's Sons, 1990) and John Dingas, *Our Man in Panama: How General Noriega Used the United States and Made Millions in Dollars and Arms* (New York: Random House, 1990). An excellent scholarly account is Margaret E. Scranton, *The Noriega Years, 1981-1990* (Boulder: Lynne Rienner Publishers, 1991). Critical accounts by Panamanians include Kenneth E. Jones, *Tiempos de agonia: expulsando el dictador de Panama* (El Dorado, Panama: Focus, 1990); Ricardo Stevens, *Metamorfosis de las fuerzas armades en Panama, 1968-1986* (s. i., s. n., 1987) and Milton H. Martínez, *Panama: una crisis sin fin* (Panama: Centro de Estudios y Acción Social Panemeño, 1990). For a defense of Noriega see Medoro Lagos, *Noriega: legitmas alternativa de la causa de Panama* (Panama City: Editoria Renovación, 1988).

UNITED STATES-PANAMANIAN RELATIONS

Relations between Panama and the United States have focused upon the canal and related issues. While most of the literature is critical of United States policies, Michael L. Conniff's *Panama and the United States: The Forced Alliance* (Athens, Ga.: University of Georgia Press, 1992) presents a more balanced picture. Walter LaFeber, *The Panama Canal: The Crisis in Historical Perspective* (New York: Oxford University Press, 1978), concludes that the United States manipulated the Panamanians for their own purposes. Two competent surveys through 1940 are William McCain's *The United States and the Republic of Panama* (Durham: Duke University Press, 1947) and Norman J. Padelford's, *The Panama Canal in Peace and War* (New York: The MacMillan Company, 1942). Sheldon B. Liss, *The Canal: Aspects of United States-Panamanian Relations* (Notre Dame, Ind.: University of Notre Dame Press, 1967) places the canal issue in the Cold War context from 1945 to 1960. Lawrence O. Ealy's *Yanqui Politics and the Isthmian Canal* (University Park, Pa.: Pennsylvania State University Press, 1971) provides a good account of the U. S. political debates over the canal.

The Panamanian side is represented by Ernesto Castillero Pimentel, *Panama y los Estados Unidos* (Panama City: Editoria Humidad, 1953) Ricardo J. Alfaro, *Medío siglo de relaciones entre Panama y los Estados Unidos* (Panama City: Secretaria de Información de la Presidencia del la Republica, 1959) Isiás B. Ballesteros, *El drama de Panama y America, neustras relaciones con los Estados Unidos* (Panama City: Imprenta nacional, 1965) and Gregorio Selser, *Panama autodeterminación versus intervención de Estados Unidos* (Mexico City: Program de Estudios de Centroamérica del Centro de

Investigaciónes y Docencia Economicas, 1988). Although dated, the best work in English that explains the Panamanian perspective is Lawrence O. Ealy's *The Republic of Panama in World Affairs, 1903-1950* (Philadelphia: The University of Pennsylvania Press, 1951). The most complete account of the United States canal interests to 1903 is David McCullough, *The Path Between the Seas: The Creation of the Panama Canal, 1870-1914* (New York: Simon and Schuster, 1977). An earlier, but equally important work is Miles DuVal, *From Cadiz to Cathay: The Story of the Long Diplomatic Struggle for the Panama Canal* (New York: Greenwood Press, 1968). An excellent study of U. S. relations with Colombia during the nineteenth century is F. Taylor Parks, *Colombia and the United States, 1765-1934* (Durham: Duke University Press, 1934). For the Colombian side of the Panama canal issue see José Uribe, *Colombia y Estados Unidos de América*, (Bogotá: Imprenta Nacional, 1933). Still the most important work for understanding United States-British relations in the nineteenth century is Mary W. Williams, *Anglo-American Isthmian Diplomacy, 1815-1915* (Washington, D. C.: American Historical Association, 1916). An excellent analysis of the U. S. response to the French project is Walter E. Lowrie, "France, the United States and the deLesseps Canal: Renewed Rivalry in the Western Hemisphere, 1879-1889," Ph. D. diss., Syracuse University, 1975. Jackson H. Crowell's "The United States and a Central American Canal, 1869-1877," *Hispanic American Historical Review* 49 (February, 1969), 27-52, discusses the growing North American interest in a transisthmian route. The pressure exerted by U. S. businessmen for a transisthmian canal is illustrated by Ralph D. Bald, Jr.'s "The Development of Expansionist Sentiment in the United States, 1885-1895, as Reflected in the Periodical Literature," Ph. D. diss., University of Pittsburgh, 1973. A broader perspective is provided by Alfred C. Richard's, "The Panama Canal in American National Consciousness, 1870-1922," Ph. D. diss., Boston University, 1966. The security angle is examined by William R. Adams, "Strategy, Diplomacy and Isthmian Canal Security, 1880-1917," Ph. D. diss., Florida State University, 1974.

The rapprochement between Britain and the United States that resulted in the second Hay-Pauncefote Treaty, which paved the way for the U. S. canal project, is examined by Charles S. Campbell, Jr., *Anglo-American Understanding, 1898-1903* (Baltimore: Johns Hopkins University Press, 1957). An excellent analysis of the events that led to the rejection of the Nicaraguan route and selection of the Panama site is found in Dwight C. Minor, *The Fight for the Panama Route: The Story of the Spooner Act and the Hay-Herrán Treaty* (New York, Octagon Books, 1971).

In addition to the materials noted above that deal with the Colombian-Panamanian independence struggle and appropriate chapters in the general diplomatic surveys, much has been written about the United States role in the independence of Panama. Richard H. Collin's *Theodore Roosevelt's Caribbean: The Panama Canal, the Monroe Doctrine and the Latin American Context* (Baton Rouge: Louisiana State University Press, 1990) is the most recent analysis. David Healy puts Panama into the wider perspective of Caribbean policy in *Drive to Hegemony: The United States and the Caribbean, 1898-1917* (Madison: University of Wisconsin, 1988).

Among the most indispensable sources dealing with the finer points of U. S. policy are: John Major, "Who Wrote the Hay-Bunau-Varilla Convention," *Diplomatic History* 8 (Spring, 1984), 115-123; Charles D. Ameringer, "Philippe Bunau-Varilla: New Light on the Panama Canal Treaty," *Hispanic American Historical Review* 46 (February, 1966), 28-52; Charles D. Ameringer, "The Panama Canal Lobby of Philippe Bunau-Varilla and William Nelson Cromwell," *American Historical Review* 67 (January, 1963), 346-363; and James F. Vivian, "The 'Taking' of the Panama Canal Zone, Myth and Reality," *Diplomatic History* 4 (Winter, 1980), 95-100.

Panama's immediate concern with sovereignty over the Canal Zone was examined by Harmodio Arias, *The Panama Canal: A Study in International Law and Diplomacy* (London: P. S. King and Son, 1911). A broader perspective of the sovereignty issue is found in Ralph E. Minger's "Panama, the Canal Zone and Titular Sovereignty," *Western Political Quarterly* 14 (March, 1961), 544-554, and Ricardo J. Alfaro's "America's Troubled Canal: Panamanians are Questioning Our Sovereignty in the Zone," *Fortune* 55 (February, 1957). 129-132.

For insights into relations immediately after the canal opened to world traffic in 1914 see George W. Baker, "The Wilson Administration in Panama, 1913-1921," *Journal of Inter-American Studies* 8 (April 1966), 279-283 and Celesttino Andrés Araúz, "Belisario Porras y las relacionnes de Panama con los Estados Unidos," *Cuadernos Universitarios* 3 (June, 1988), 13-16. The negotiations that resulted in the proposed 1926 treaty are explained by Thomas M. Leonard, "The United States and Panama: Negotiating the Aborted 1926 Treaty," *Mid-America* 61 (October, 1979), 189-203. Fabian Verlarde's *Análises de nuevo tratado* (Panama City: Star & Herald, 1927) explains Panama's opposition to the proposed 1926 treaty. A contemporary analysis of relations can be found in "Panama," *Foreign Policy Information Service* 3 (January 20, 1928), 354-359.

The advent of the Good Neighbor Policy in 1933 brought changes in U. S. policy toward Panama. John Major, "F. D. R. and Panama," *Historical Journal* 28 (March, 1985), 357-377 and Lester D. Langley,

"Negotiating New Treaties with Panama, 1936," *Hispanic American Historical Review* 48 (May, 1968), 220-233 discuss aspects of the new policy. During the negotiations for the 1936 treaties, the Panamanians sought, for the first time, economic concessions. That issue is examined by Thomas M. Leonard, "The Commissary Issue in United States-Panamanian Relations, *The Americas* 30 (July, 1973), 83-109.

At the same time the United States was changing its hemispheric policy, European and Asian war clouds raised new issues about the canal's defense. The U. S. story is told by Almon R. Wright, "The United States and Panama, 1933-1949," United States Department of State Research Project 499 (Washington, D. C.: Government Printing Office, 1952). A scholarly examination is John A. Cooley, "The United States and the Panama Canal, 1933-1947," Ph. D. diss., Ohio State University, 1972. Important studies of prewar period include, Lester D. Langley, "The World Crisis and the Good Neighbor Policy in Panama, 1936-1941," *The Americas,* 24 (October, 1967), 137-152, and Donald A. Yerxa, "The United States Navy and the Caribbean Sea, 1914-1941," Ph. D. diss., University of Maine, 1982. Broader studies of the canal security issue are found in David G. Haglund, *Latin America and the Transformation of U.S. Strategic Thought* (Albuquerque: University of New Mexico Press, 1984) and Stetson Conn and Byron Fairchild, *The Western Hemisphere: The Framework of Hemisphere Defense* (Washington, D. C.: Government Printing Office, 1960).

With the end of World War II, the U. S. needed to reassess the canal's importance, while Panama placed greater responsibility upon the Canal Zone for its misfortunes. For the defense issue see Almon R. Wright, above, and John Major, "Wasting Asset: The U. S. Reassessment of the Panama Canal 1945-1949," *Journal of Strategic Studies* 3 (September, 1980), 123-146. For a discussion of the canal during the ambience of the early Cold War see John Major, " 'Pro mundi beneficio'? The Panama Canal as an International Issue, 1943-1948," *Review of International Studies*, 9 (February, 1983), 17-34.

Also, following World War II, the Panamanians became more sophisticated in articulating their demands. This is seen in William A. Naughton, "Panama Versus the United States: A Case Study in Small State Diplomacy," Ph. D. diss., American University, 1972; Kent J. Minor, "United States-Panamanian Relations, 1958-1973," Ph. D. diss., Case Western Reserve University, 1974; and Lester D. Langley, " U. S. -Panamanian Relations Since 1941," *Journal of Inter-American Studies* 12 (July, 1970), 339-366.

The 1964 tragedy is anticipated in Mercer D. Tate, "The Panama Canal and Political Partnership," *Journal of Politics* 25 (February, 1963), 119-138. The events of 1964 are reported by the International Commission of Jurists noted above. A criticism of U. S. policy at this point is J. Fred Rippy, "The U.S and Panama: The High Cost of Appeasement," *Inter-American Economic Affairs* 17 (Spring, 1964), 87-94. The best account of U. S. policy toward Panama during the Kennedy-Johnson years is William J. Jorden, *Panama Odyssey* (Austin: University of Texas Press, 1984).

Contrasting accounts of the treaty negotiations during the 1960s and 1970s are found in David N. Farnsworth and James W. McKenney, *U. S.-Panamanian Relations, 1903-1978* (Boulder: Westview Press, 1983) and Rómulo Escobar Bethancourt, *Torrijos: Colonia americana no!* (Bogotá: Carlos Valencia, 1981). The Carter administration position is explained in Jimmy Carter, *Keeping the Faith* (New York: Bantam Books, 1982) and Cyrus Vance, *Hard Choices* (New York: Simon and Shuster, 1983). A contemporary criticism of the 1968 proposed canal treaties can be found in Mercer D. Tate and E. H. Allen, "Proposed New Treaties for the Panama Canal," *International Affairs* 45 (April, 1969), 269-278. Julio Yau has made three important analyses of the canal treaty process: "El anuncio conjunto Tack-Kissinger," *Tareas* 30 (January-April, 1975), 7-34; La política exterior de Panama," *Desarrollo indoamericano* 27 (April, 1975), 49-58; and "Los tratados Torrijos-Carter algunas lecciones," *Diálogo social* 97 (February, 1978), 18-21. The U. S. treaty ratification debate is discussed by J. Michael Hogan, *The Panama Canal in American Politics* (Carbondale, Ill: Southern Illinois University Press, 1986), and George D. Moffett, III, *The Limits of Victory: The Ratification of the Panama Canal Treaties* (Ithaca, N. Y.: Cornell University Press, 1985). An historical analysis of the treaties is Thomas M. Leonard, "The 1977 Panama Canal Treaties in Historical Perspective," *Journal of Caribbean Studies* 2 (Autumn-Winter, 1981), 190-209. A description of the application of the 1977 Panama Canal treaties can be found in John P. Augelli, "The Panama Canal Area in Transition," Hanover, N.H., American Universities Field Staff Reports, nos. 3-4 (1981). After 1981, the canal issue became subsumed in relations between the United States and Manuel Noriega and one should consult the literature noted above on the Panamanian head of state.

The December 1989 invasion of Panama is the subject of many books. Among the most important are: Rebecca Grant, *Operation Just Cause and the U. S. Policy Process* (Santa Monica, CA: Rand, 1991) Thomas M. Donnelly, *Operation Just Cause: The Storming of Panama* (New York: Lexington Books, 1991) and Kevin Buckley, *Panama: The Whole Story* (New York: Simon and Shuster, 1991).

To keep abreast of events in Panama since the invasion two excellent monthly news digests are *Mesoamérica* published in English and Spanish in San José, Costa Rica, and the London based publication *Regional Report: Mexico and Central America*.